Junior Skill Builders

READING
in
15 Minutes a Day

LearningExpress®

NEW YORK

Library of Congress Cataloging-in-Publication Data:
Junior skill builders : reading in 15 minutes a day.
    p. cm.
  ISBN: 978-1-57685-661-1
  1. Reading (Middle school)   2. Reading (Secondary)   3. English language—Grammar—Study and teaching (Middle school)   4. English language—Grammar—Study and teaching (Secondary)   I. LearningExpress (Organization)   II. Title: Reading in 15 minutes a day.
  LB1632.J86 2008
  428.4071'2—dc22   2008020199

Printed in the United States of America

10 9 8 7 6 5 4 3 2 1

First Edition

For more information or to place an order, contact LearningExpress at:
  2 Rector Street
  26th Floor
  New York, NY 10006

Or visit us at:
  www.learnatest.com

CONTENTS

I N T R O D U C T I O N

CAN YOU SPARE 15 minutes a day for 30 days? If so, *Junior Skill Builders: Reading in 15 Minutes a Day* can help you improve your reading comprehension skills.

Just what is reading comprehension? Here's a clue: *Understanding* is a synonym for *comprehension*. So, as I'm sure you figured out, *reading comprehension* means, "understanding what you read." Not everyone does, you know. If you ask some people to tell you about a book or article they read, they often say, "I'm not really sure—I didn't get it!" Well, this book will help you definitely "get it" every time you read, whether it's an ad or a full-length novel!

THE BOOK AT A GLANCE

What's in the book? First, there's this introduction, in which you'll discover some things good readers do to get more out of what they read. Next, there's a pretest that lets you find out what you already know about the topics in the book's lessons—you may be surprised by how much you already know. Then, there are 30 lessons. After the last one, there's a posttest. Take it to reveal how much you've learned and improved your skills!

The lessons are divided into four sections:

1. **Build Your Vocabulary:** *The Wonder of Words*
   Figuring out the meaning of unknown words
2. **Variety in Reading:** *What's to Read?*
   Recognizing the characteristics of different kinds, or genres, of writing
3. **Organization of Text:** *Putting the Words Together*
   Identifying various text structures an author can use to present ideas
4. **Elements of Literature:** *The Facts about Fiction*
   Understanding the basics and other devices authors use to make stories more interesting

Each section has a series of lessons. Each lesson explains one comprehension skill, then presents reading selections and questions so that you can practice that skill.

BECOME AN ACTIVE READER

Active readers are people who "get it." They really understand what an author is thinking, saying, and trying to get across in the text. Here are a few things active readers do. As you read this list of some things active readers do, you may discover that you're already one!

1. **Preview** what you are about to read.
   Read the selection title and look over any pictures and captions. Skim the text. Ask yourself: *What did the author think was important enough to show in a picture? Why did the author choose to put that word in boldface, or darker, text?*
2. **Predict** what the selection will be about.
   What do you think the selection is about? Write your prediction on a sticky note and attach it to the selection. As you read, look for information to confirm your prediction.

3. **Set a purpose** for reading.

    Ask yourself: *Why am I planning to read this? What do I want to get from it?* Maybe it's assigned reading for class and you want to find facts so you can answer questions. Maybe you need to read directions that tell you how to do something. Or maybe you just want to read for enjoyment. Knowing *why* you're reading can help you get what you want from the text.

4. **Ask** questions to guide your reading.

    Ask some 5Ws and an H question: *Who? What? When? Where? Why?* and *How?* For example: *Where do the characters live? Why did they choose to do what they just did?* As you read, look for answers. They might be right there, explained in the text. Or you might have to put details from the text together to figure out the answer to your question.

5. **Note** what's important.

    As you read, highlight or underline key words and ideas. Ask yourself: *Is this word or detail really important or is it just kind of interesting?* Make sure you identify and highlight or underline only the most important ones. And write your personal reactions to what you read in the margins or on sticky notes by the text. How you react to what you read is very important.

6. **Clear** the way.

    As you read, stop if you're confused. Circle unfamiliar words or phrases, then reread the text. That may make the meaning clear. If it doesn't, check nearby words and pictures for clues to the meaning. And tap into your own personal knowledge. Ask yourself: *Have I ever read anything else about this subject before? Do I know a word or phrase that means about the same thing?* Try that word or phrase in the text to see if it makes sense. If you're still confused, just read on. Maybe you'll find the answer there!

7. **Ask** questions to understand the author.

    Try to figure out how the author thinks and what he or she is trying to communicate to you. Ask questions like: *Did the author write this to inform me, entertain me, or persuade me to do something? Is the writing funny, sad, friendly, scary, or serious? Why did the author choose this particular word to describe the character? Why did the author have the character react like that? Does the author tell both sides of the story?*

8. **Return, review, and reword**

When you finish reading, review your sticky notes and high-lighted or underlined text. This will quickly remind you not only of the most important ideas, but also of how those ideas are connected. Finally, state what the selection is about in your own words.

Each of these points is covered again later in the book. But for now, practice being an active reader as you take the pretest that follows!

P R E T E S T

THIS PRETEST HAS 30 multiple-choice questions about topics covered in the book's 30 lessons. Find out how much you already know about the topics; then, you'll discover what you still need to learn. Read each question carefully. Circle your answers in the book if the book belongs to you. If it doesn't, write the numbers 1–30 on a paper and record your answers there.

When you finish the test, check the answers on page 16. Don't worry if you didn't get all the answers right. If you did, you wouldn't need this book! If you do have an incorrect answer, check the number of the lesson(s) listed with the right answer. That's where you'll find more about that skill.

If you get a lot of questions right, you can probably spend less time using this book. If you get a lot wrong, you may need to spend a few more minutes a day to really improve your reading comprehension.

FIRST PEOPLES OF THE NORTHEAST

Read the selection, and then answer the questions that follow.

(1)   About 10,000 years ago, the first hunter-gatherers arrived on the east coast of what is now the United States. They found forest-covered mountains and valleys, and hundreds of streams and lakes—natural resources that could meet their needs.

Using Resources

(2)   The trees provided supplies for building. Forest and water animals, and nuts and berries on land, provided food. People used the soil and water to grow their own food. They planted corn, or *maize*, and pumpkin, squash, and beans. Summer sun and rain made the crops thrive. Soon people didn't need to be constantly on the move in search of food. So they settled down and built permanent homes.

(3)   Villages of dome-shaped wigwams sprang up near lakes and streams. Each wigwam was made by first sticking thin, bendable trees into the ground to form a circle. Next, the poles were bent inward and tied together at the top. More thin branches were wrapped and tied around the poles, leaving space for a door and a smoke hole above the center, where an indoor fire would be. Finally, the whole structure was covered with tree bark.

(4)   The men also built a larger, rectangular, council house and a lodge to use for ceremonies. Then they built a stockade around the whole village. The fence helped protect the villagers from enemy attack.

Everyone Works

(5)   Most of the year, the men hunted in swiftly moving birch-bark canoes. But in winter, the hunters needed sleds and snowshoes to get across the snowy ground. The women raised and prepared the food, even tapping maple trees for the sweet syrup. They made deerskin clothing, adding colored porcupine-quill designs, and pottery jars for cooking and storing food.

(6)   After the fall harvest, everyone helped prepare for winter. They dried the crops, and meat and fish from the hunt, in the sun. Then they hung them from the ceilings of their wigwams or stored them in underground pits. Young and old worked together to assure there would be enough food to last until spring.

1. The author probably wrote this to
   a. inform readers about early settlers on the east coast.
   b. teach readers how to make a wigwam
   c. entertain readers with a scary tale.
   d. persuade readers to visit New England.

2. Which text feature does the author use to divide the article into sections?
   a. contents
   b. glossary
   c. index
   d. subheads

3. As used in the selection, the meaning of the word *spring* is
   a. metal coil.
   b. leap forward.
   c. season of the year.
   d. bounce.

4. The people were able to settle down and build homes because
   a. they had modern tools to help them.
   b. they didn't need to keep moving in search of food.
   c. there were not too many rocks in the region.
   d. they could travel across the ocean by boat.

5. The author organizes the ideas in this article by
   a. telling a problem and suggesting solutions.
   b. ranking ideas in the order of their importance.
   c. the chronological order in which things happened.
   d. comparing and contrasting things.

A CONTEST OF STRENGTH

An Aesop's Fable Retold

Read the story, and then answer the questions that follow.

(1)   Wind and Sun were both important weather makers, but each thought he
      was more powerful than the other was. Wind argued that his great strength
      made him more powerful. Sun argued that the ability to persuade gave him
      greater power.

(2) "Let's have a contest to prove who's more powerful!" suggested Wind boastfully. Far below, he saw a man in a warm, winter coat walking along the road. "Whoever can make that man take off his coat will be more powerful," said Wind with a smile. "I'll go first."

(3) Now Wind knew that when he blew, leaves flew through the air and trees bent. It should be easy to blow a man's coat off! So Wind blew, gently at first, then harder and harder. But the harder he blew, the more the shivering man pulled his coat around him!

(4) "My turn," said Sun, and he began to send warm rays toward the man below. Soon the man unbuttoned his coat. Sun glowed brighter and the man became uncomfortable in the heat. Before long, he took off the coat!

(5) Wind sighed. "I guess you win. You're more powerful."

(6) Sun just beamed. And all day he was as busy as a bee, lighting the sky until it was time for Moon to take over!

6. The theme of this fable is
  a. "Everyone has some kind of strength."
  b. "Don't count your chickens before they hatch."
  c. "Don't cry over spilt milk."
  d. "Gentle persuasion is better than force."

7. Which human characteristics did the writer NOT give Wind or Sun?
  a. the ability to smile
  b. the ability to walk
  c. the ability to talk
  d. the ability to laugh

8. The phrase *busy as a bee* is an example of a
  a. simile.
  b. metaphor.
  c. hyperbole.
  d. idiom.

9. The clue that this is told from the third-person point of view is the use of
  a. the pronoun *I.*
  b. the noun *coat.*
  c. the pronoun *he.*
  d. the verb *blew.*

10. Describing Wind as *arrogant* means he was
   a. full of self-importance.
   b. full of thanks.
   c. full of wonder.
   d. full of humility.

11. You can infer that when Sun just beamed at the end of the story,
   a. he knew he was better than Moon.
   b. he felt he didn't have to say anything because he'd won.
   c. he didn't want to hurt the man's feelings.
   d. he wanted to keep the bees warm.

12. What is the main conflict in the story?
   a. Sun wants Moon to light the sky.
   b. Wind wants to make a big tree bend.
   c. The man doesn't know which way to go on the road.
   d. The Wind and Sun need to get the man's coat off.

WILD HORSES

Read the poem, and then answer the questions that follow.

> Proudly he runs free
> Through the grasses growing high,
> Then suddenly catches a sound
> On the wind that's passing by.
> He knows that sound means danger,
> So he neighs a resonant cry
> To warn the other wild ones
> Who are grazing there nearby.
> Then off they all go racing,
> Their hooves beating the ground,
> And all that I can hear
> Is a rumbling, thundering sound!

13. You can tell this is a poem because it has
   a. words that describe action.
   b. information about horses.
   c. a rhyme scheme.
   d. lines for actors to say.

14. Which word in the poem means the same as *ringing*?
   a. rumbling
   b. thundering
   c. beating
   d. resonant

15. Which group of words from the poem is the best example of imagery?
   a. "He knows"
   b. "other wild ones"
   c. "rumbling, thundering"
   d. "and all that"

THE WITCH AT MURPHY'S POND

Read the story, and then answer the questions that follow.

(1)   "I don't get it, Pete," Janet said to her cousin. "Why do you fish at Murphy's Pond if old Mrs. Murphy is a witch?"

(2)   "The fishing's great . . . and the old Murphy house is over a hill behind the pond," Pete replied. "We'll be okay . . . as long as we stay away from the house," he continued in a hushed voice. "They say kids who go into that house are never seen again!"

(3)   After they got to the pond, witches were forgotten. Pete sat on the old dock and threw out his line. Suddenly Janet saw something shimmering in the water and leaned over for a closer look. The rotting wood of the dock broke under her! "H-e-l-l-p!" she screamed as she splashed down into the dark, cold water.

(4)   Pete jumped in to help her. "Quiet down!" he panted as they got to the rocky shore. "You're not hurt. If you keep hollering, you'll wake the witch!" Then he yelped, "OUCH-H-H!" and lifted his foot. There was a deep cut on the bottom of his foot from a sharp rock!

(5)   "Oh, Pete, you're hurt!" Janet cried. "I'll go for . . ." But before she could say Help, she saw an old woman coming toward them. Without a word, the woman picked up Pete and carried him up the hill. A cold, wet, and confused Janet followed. She was frightened but had a strange feeling the old woman meant no harm.

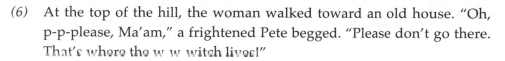

(6) At the top of the hill, the woman walked toward an old house. "Oh, p-p-please, Ma'am," a frightened Pete begged. "Please don't go there. That's where the w w witch lives!"

(7) "That is my home, young man," the woman said softly. "Do not be afraid." At the front door, she said to Janet. "Please open the door." Janet did, and the three went inside. Mrs. Murphy gently put Pete on a couch, then disappeared into another room.

(8) Mrs. Murphy returned with warm blankets, which she wrapped around the two cold and wet cousins. Then she carefully cleaned and bandaged Pete's foot. The still-frightened boy squeezed his eyes shut every time she came near him. Finally, she offered Pete and Janet some freshly baked bread and glasses of milk. They began to understand that Mrs. Murphy was a very kind . . . but very lonely . . . woman.

(9) Pete reached out and touched Mrs. Murphy's hand. "I'm Pete, and this is my cousin, Janet," he said. "Thank you for helping us."

(10) Mrs. Murphy smiled shyly. She seemed to enjoy their company but said sadly, "You'd best be on your way. It's getting late."

(11) Before they left, Mrs. Murphy reminded Pete to have a doctor check the cut and they promised to return to see her another day. She waved good-bye until they were out of sight. "Oh, Pete, she's so nice!" said Janet. "How could you have thought she was a witch?"

(12) Pete smiled as he hobbled along beside her. "Well, she still might be," he said, and as Janet gasped, he added, "but she'd be the good kind!"

16. Which words from the text are NOT an example of foreshadowing?
   a. "We'll be okay . . . as long as we stay away from the house."
   b. Pete stood on the old dock and threw out his line.
   c. Janet saw something shimmering in the water.
   d. "If you keep hollering, you'll wake the witch!"

17. Which homophones were in the story?
   a. *witch* and *which*
   b. *threw* and *through*
   c. *seen* and *scene*
   d. *there* and *their*

18. Which was NOT part of the story's plot?
  a. Pete and Janet go to Murphy's Pond.
  b. Janet falls into the water.
  c. Mrs. Murphy drives Pete and Janet home.
  d. Pete and Janet both get wet.

19. This selection is an example of
  a. fiction.
  b. poetry.
  c. nonfiction.
  d. drama.

20. A story has to include a setting because
  a. without a setting, there would be no characters.
  b. the story would be too short.
  c. the reader needs to know when and where the story takes place.
  d. the author needs to tell who the main character is.

21. What is the main tone of the selection?
  a. silly
  b. exciting
  c. mocking
  d. whimsical

22. The most likely conclusion you can draw from the story is that
  a. there are witches living near Murphy's Pond.
  b. the author was once frightened by a witch.
  c. witches don't like young people.
  d. just because someone tells you something doesn't make it true.

A CLASS ACT

Read the selection, and then answer the questions that follow.

(1)   First of all, let me start by saying that even though I had to recite an original poem in front of the class Tuesday, I was cool . . . well, pretty cool about it. On Monday night my little sister said, "I hate talking in front of the class. Aren't you scared?"

(2)   "I have no trepidation!" I had replied, matter-of-factly. I love using big words with her because I know she'll run to look them up in the dictionary, so it's a win-win situation. I get rid of her and she gets a bigger vocabulary, like finding out that *trepidation* means "fear."

(3)   Tuesday morning, Mom fixed my favorite breakfast: pancakes. She flipped a few golden-brown circles off the griddle with a spatula and stacked them on my plate. As usual, I took a big bite. And as usual, sticky syrup dripped off the pancakes and onto my clean shirt.

(4)   "Oh, you are such a pig," my sister mumbled as she rolled her eyes at me.

(5)   "It's okay, Honey, you're probably just nervous about your poem," said Mom sympathetically.

(6)   I didn't answer either one of them; I just raced to my room for a clean shirt! I wanted to look my best. I barely made it out the door before the bus pulled away! *What a start to my day*, I thought. *Let's hope things get better.*

(7)   Well, to make a long story short, I did recite my original poem that morning, but with a bit of trepidation. The kid who read his poem ahead of me was really good, I mean, he really knew how to put words together on paper and read them with meaning! Then it was my turn. As I stood up, my BFF Pat whispered, "You'll be great!" And you know what? I kind of was! I even surprised myself. Our teacher, Mr. Briggs, videotaped the presentations and played them back so we could evaluate our work, and I was good . . . I mean really good. As I went out the door at the end of class, Mr. Briggs even stopped me and said, "Hope you're trying out for the school play this spring. It's Shakespeare. I'm directing and I think you'd be a really good actor. The auditions will be in three weeks."

(8)   So, I went to the auditions and . . . well, that's another story. Let's just say I am now a thespian!

23. To help readers know that *thespian* means "actor," the author uses context clues like
   a. *poem* and *presentation*.
   b. *play* and *audition*.
   c. *trepidation* and *teacher*.
   d. *syrup* and *recite*.

24. Which antonym pair is NOT used in the selection?
   a. *short* and *long*
   b. *clean* and *dirty*
   c. *up* and *down*
   d. *front* and *back*

25. The denotation of *pig* is "a four-legged, young swine." In this selection, the connotation of *pig* is
   a. "a really smart person."
   b. "a dirty, messy person."
   c. "a shy, sweet person."
   d. "a helpful, kind person."

26. With which topic would you most likely use the term *spatula*?
   a. medicine
   b. airplanes
   c. cooking
   d. geography

27. Which is the best one-sentence summary for this story?
   a. The narrator teaches a younger sibling some new words.
   b. The narrator is preparing to read an original poem aloud.
   c. The narrator is invited to be in the school play because of a good poetry presentation.
   d. The narrator helps the teacher direct the school play.

THE HIGH POINTS OF LIFE ON EARTH

Read the article and the chart, and then answer the questions that follow.

(1)   Mountains make up one-fourth of Earth's surface. But what exactly is a mountain? Scientifically speaking, it's a land formation at an altitude of at least 2,000 feet above its surroundings.

(2)   Mountains come in various heights. One mountain may look like a dwarf compared to Africa's Mt. Kilimanjaro. But that looks small compared to Asia's giant Mt. Everest. Each of Earth's seven continents has a high point called the "Seven Summits."

Continent	Mountain	Height
Asia	Mt. Everest	29,035 ft.
South America	Mt. Aconcagua	22,834 ft.
North America	Mt. McKinley (Denali)	20,320 ft.
Africa	Mt. Kilimanjaro	19,340 ft.
Europe	Elbrus	18,510 ft.
Antarctica	Vinson Massif	16,066 ft.
Australia	Kosciusko	7,310 ft.

28. What data does the chart show?
   a. cities where mountain peaks are found
   b. when each mountain peak was discovered
   c. heights of all mountains in the Alps
   d. the names and heights of the Seven Summits

29. The first sentence is a fact, not an opinion because
   a. it mentions Earth, and Earth is real.
   b. it is short.
   c. you can check it to prove it is true.
   d. it's what the author thinks.

30. Which is the main idea of this article?
   a. Mountains are found everywhere in the world, except in Australia.
   b. To be a mountain, land must be 2,000 feet higher than the surrounding area.
   c. The world's highest mountain is in the United States.
   d. Earth's mountains can be seen from outer space.

ANSWERS

If you miss a question, look for help with that topic in the lesson(s) listed.

1. a (Lesson 9)
2. d (Lesson 11)
3. c (Lesson 1)
4. b (Lesson 17)
5. c (Lessons 14, 15, 16, 19)
6. d (Lesson 26)
7. b (Lesson 29)
8. a (Lessons 29, 30)
9. c (Lesson 25)
10. a (Lessons 4, 23)
11. b (Lesson 20)
12. d (Lesson 24)
13. c (Lesson 8)
14. d (Lesson 3)
15. c (Lesson 27)
16. b (Lesson 28)
17. d (Lesson 2)
18. c (Lesson 24)
19. a (Lesson 8)
20. c (Lesson 23)
21. b (Lesson 10)
22. d (Lesson 21)
23. b (Lesson 6)
24. d (Lesson 28)
25. b (Lesson 7)
26. c (Lesson 5)
27. c (Lesson 22)
28. d (Lesson 12)
29. c (Lesson 18)
30. b (Lesson 13)

SECTION 1

build your vocabulary

THE WONDER OF WORDS

As you read, you have to think about what all the words and groups of words mean. And sometimes you come across a word you don't know. What does it mean? You need to figure out the meaning so you can understand what the author's trying to tell you. And you want to know what it means so you can add it to your vocabulary for future use! So what can you do? Well, you could look up the word in a dictionary. Or you could ask someone to tell you what it means. But you become a better and more active reader when you figure it out for yourself. In this section of the book, you'll discover how you can do that by

- identifying words that have more than one meaning.
- distinguishing between words that sound alike but have different meanings.
- recognizing words that mean the same or the opposite.
- distinguishing between word parts.
- recognizing technical terms and jargon used by special groups.
- locating and using context clues.
- distinguishing between what a word means and what it suggests.

multiple-meaning words

> *VINZINNI: Inconceivable!*
> *INIGO: You keep using that word. I do not think*
> *it means what you think it means.*
> WILLIAM GOLDMAN (1931–),
> NOVELIST, SCREENWRITER, "THE PRINCESS BRIDE"

In this lesson, you'll discover that some words can mean more than one thing . . . it's up to you to figure out which meaning an author is using.

YOU MAY ALREADY know many words that have two or more meanings. The words are called **homonyms**, from the Greek for "same name." For example, the word *fly* is a *noun* that means "a small insect."

Example
A pesky *fly* kept buzzing by my ear!

But *fly* can also be a *verb* that means "to move through the air with wings."

Example
My brother likes to design and *fly* paper airplanes.

So which meaning does this author use in the following quote? "I wonder what they're talking about in that room? Boy, I wish I were a *fly* on the wall!"

You probably figured it out. The writer wants to be a tiny insect that people wouldn't notice as it listened to their private conversation!

Here are just a few more familiar multiple-meaning words.

Word	Meaning 1	Meaning 2
bark	growl	tree covering
bat	animal	wooden stick
bowl	dish	a sport
can	able to	container
kind	nice	type
light	lamp	not heavy
mean	unkind	suggest
play	have fun	a drama
roll	revolve	a small piece of dough
story	tale	one floor of a building
watch	look at	timepiece

PRACTICE 1: A DAY AT THE PARK

Read the selection, and then answer the questions that follow.

(1)   It's a lazy Saturday. I'm happy just hanging out . . . doing nothing. Then my little brother runs into my room and announces, "We're going to the park!"

(2)   "Have fun," I reply.

(3)   "No! Get up and get ready!" he whines, and pulls my arm. "Dad said we're going to make a day of it . . . the whole family!"

(4)   Dad drops us off by the park entrance and goes to park the car. I help Mom unload the picnic basket onto a table. She's packed a huge covered plate of sandwiches, a bowl of fruit, bags of chips, lots of cookies, and a gigantic pitcher of iced tea. Mom always makes extra "just in case . . . ," whatever that means!

(5)   "Before we eat, will you help me fly my new kite?" pleads my brother. With a sigh, I take his hand and lead him to a good spot for flying kites. Soon the kite's airborne and looping through the sky! Suddenly, it's harder to spot because it floats behind a tree.

(6)   "Is it lost forever?" asks my brother.

(7)   "No, just hiding. There . . . see . . . it's back!" I chuckle as the kite pops back into view.

(8)   "Dude!" I hear someone behind me say. "Just the guy I was looking for!" I turn to find Chris, one of my best friends.

(9)   "I thought you went to visit your uncle this weekend!" I say.

(10)   "No, he had to go away on business, so I'll catch him another time," Chris replies. "Nice kite," he adds, "but I was hoping to play ball today."

(11)   "I'm in," I answer. "We're about to stop. My brother wants Dad to push him on a swing."

(12)   So we find more friends to play ball. Suddenly, it's the last inning, the game is tied, and I'm at bat. I see Mom waving me to come for lunch, so there's nothing to do but hit a homer! I swing, hear the *crack* of the bat, and head for home plate. Then I invite the other kids to join us for lunch . . . knowing Mom had made extra! I guess this was the "just in case!"

1. What is the meaning of the word *park* as used in the first paragraph?
   a. leave a car in a parking lot
   b. sit down
   c. an open, public area of land used for recreation
   d. an arctic jacket

2. Which is NOT a meaning of *plate* as used in the story?
   a. tray
   b. dish
   c. marker for a base
   d. coat with metal

3. Which of the following words from paragraph 5 is a multiple-meaning word?
   a. pleads
   b. spot
   c. kite
   d. before

4. The meaning of *back* as used in paragraph 7 is
   a. "a piece connected to the seat of a chair."
   b. "the opposite of *front*."
   c. "to return."
   d. "to sponsor or give money to."

5. The last paragraph contains all these multiple-meaning words: *play, ball, pitcher, tied, bat, swing,* and *head.* Choose three of the words and write short sentences illustrating at least two meanings for each.

_____

_____

_____

PRACTICE 2: CROSSING OVER

Read the selection, and then answer the questions that follow.

(1) Have you ever thought about how important a bridge is? After all, without bridges, how would people get across rivers and wide gorges? Bridges are an essential part of our transportation system for moving people and goods.

(2) The first bridges were simply trees that fell or were placed across water or canyons. The wood was strong enough to bear the weight of a person or two at a time, but not for carrying heavy loads. People made bridges by stretching rope cables across an open area. In China and other places, rope bridges are still used. They're strong enough to hold people and pack animals with light loads.

(3) Later, people built arch bridges by wedging together large blocks of stone to form a half circle. Arch bridges are among the strongest and longest-lasting: Some built more than 1,500 years ago are still being used, Even today, people build arch bridges, but usually from concrete, wood, or steel.

(4) Another kind of bridge is the cantilever. It has two independent steel or concrete beams, one extending toward the center of a river from each bank. A third beam is lifted up to connect the beams. Canada's Quebec Bridge is one of the world's longest, spanning 1,800 feet (549 m) across the St. Lawrence River.

(5) A suspension bridge spans even more space with its roadway hanging from steel cables supported by massive towers. Each cable can hold thousands of pounds of weight. Probably the most familiar suspension bridge is California's Golden Gate, with a main span of 4,200 feet (1,280 m). When completed in 1937, it was the world's longest, but in 1964, New York's Verrazano-Narrows Bridge beat that with a span of 4,260 feet

(1,298 m). Then in 1981, England's Humber Bridge beat that with a span of 4,626 feet (1,410 m). And since 1998, Japan's Akashi-Kaikyo Bridge has held the record, with a span of 1,991 feet (6,529 m). Will that record be beaten? Stay tuned!

6. What is the meaning of the word *bridge* as used in the article?
    a. the upper bony part of the nose
    b. the part of a ship where the captain works
    c. a card game
    d. pathway structure over a river or valley

7. Which is NOT a meaning of *bear* as used in the story?
    a. hold
    b. carry
    c. furry mammal
    d. support

8. What is the meaning of the word *beam* as used in the article?
    a. long piece of heavy wood or metal used in construction
    b. width of a ship at its widest part
    c. ray of light
    d. smile

9. Which of the following words from the last paragraph is a multiple-meaning word?
    a. familiar
    b. record
    c. steel
    d. since

10. The meaning of *still* as used in the article is
    a. "quiet."
    b. "unmoving."
    c. "calm."
    d. "even now."

11. What is the meaning of the word *light* as used in the second paragraph?
    a. beam
    b. bright
    c. not heavy
    d. pale

PRACTICE 3: MAKING THINGS MOVE

Read this selection, and then answer the questions that follow.

(1)   Did you know that whatever you do, forces are at work on you? That's *right*. Forces keep your feet on the ground when you stand. Forces keep you sitting on a chair without slipping off. And a force guarantees that if you jump up, you're going to come down! Without forces you couldn't hold a *pen* to write, no matter whether you use your *right* or left! In the world of forces, things spin, stretch, twist, and *fly*, but only if something or someone applies a push or pull!

(2)   Here on Earth, gravity pulls anything at or near the surface toward the center of the planet. Things have weight because of gravity's pull. The greater the pull, the more an object weighs. We use *scales* to measure weight. When you *step* on a scale, the numbers tell how much force Earth's gravity is pulling between you and the planet itself.

12. What is the meaning of the word *pen* as used in the first paragraph?
   a. cage
   b. writing tool
   c. scribble
   d. corral

13. Which is NOT a meaning of the word *step*?
   a. stair
   b. stage or point of directions
   c. stride
   d. high

14. Which is the meaning of *scales* as used in the passage?
   a. hard pieces that cover an animal's body
   b. climbs a steep, rocky hill
   c. machines for weighing things
   d. draws in relative proportion

ANSWERS

1. a
2. d
3. b
4. c
5. Here are sample sentences:

> I'm in a play. / Please play that song again.
> The prince danced at the ball. / I hit the ball.
> Fill the pitcher with cream. / He's a baseball pitcher.
> She tied the bow. / The score is tied.
> I bat left-handed. / The bat flew away.
> Sit on this swing. / Swing your arms like this.
> My head hurts. / Let's head home.

6. d
7. c
8. a
9. b
10. d
11. c
12. b
13. d
14. c

words that sound or look alike

In the theatre, you can be seen or in a scene,
but don't confuse your objective!

S. A. CONSODINE (1931–   )
AMERICAN PLAYWRIGHT, ACTRESS, DIRECTOR

In this lesson, you'll discover that some words are *pronounced* the same but spelled differently and have different meanings, and some words are *spelled* the same but pronounced differently and have different meanings.

IN LESSON 1, you identified homonyms that sounded and were spelled alike, but had different meanings. In this lesson, you'll find **homophones** ("same sound") and **homographs** ("same writing").

Homophones *sound* the same but are spelled differently and have different meanings. As you read, don't let the homophones confuse you.

Examples
sees, seas, seize
for, four, fore
through, threw
toe, tow

Homographs are *spelled* the same but are pronounced differently and have different meanings. As you read, you need to figure out which pronunciation and meaning is used. The rest of the sentence usually lets you know.

Examples

The *wind* is blowing! *Wind* the balloon string around your finger.

In the apartment where I *live*, they don't allow *live* animals.

Separate your laundry. Put dark and light clothes in *separate* piles.

PRACTICE 1: A LONG JOURNEY

Read the selection, and then answer the questions that follow.

(1)   Dull Knife, a leader of the Cheyenne, was born *in* Montana. His *real* name was Morning Star. He got his nickname when his knife failed to *break through* his enemy's tough, buffalo-hide armor.

(2)   *In* 1876, the Cheyenne helped defeat General Custer and his U.S. troops. Other soldiers pursued the Cheyenne, and a year later, the Native Americans surrendered. They were *sent* to a reservation in Oklahoma, *where* the army promised *there* was a *herd* of buffalo *for* hunting. *There* wasn't, and many Cheyenne *died* of starvation.

(3)   Dull Knife asked permission *to* take his people home. *But* the army took over a year to "think it over," and more Cheyenne *died*. Dull Knife *knew* he had to *rebel*. So the *rebel* leader and 300 of his people escaped from the reservation and headed *for* Montana, 1,000 miles away. When they crossed into Nebraska, soldiers *there* ordered Dull Knife and his people to return *to* the Oklahoma reservation. Dull Knife refused. "*I* will never go back, "he said. "*You* may kill me *here*, but *you* cannot make me go back!"

(4)   The soldiers wondered why Dull Knife *would resent* being *resent, or sent back* to Oklahoma. They tried *to* force him *to* agree *to* go. They *threw him* and his people *into* a freezing building with *no* food *or* water *for* three days. *But* the Cheyenne *would not* give up. Instead, they climbed out windows and escaped!

(5)   The soldiers chased the Cheyenne. *Some* were killed *or* captured, *but some* escaped, including Dull Knife and his family. They walked *for* 18 days, with only tree bark and their own moccasins *to* eat! At last, they reached Montana, where sympathetic settlers had *heard* what the Cheyenne did to survive. The people asked the government *to* set up a *new* Cheyenne reservation *in* Montana. Many Cheyenne still *live there* today.

1. What does *resent* mean the first time it's used in the fourth paragraph?
   a. sent again
   b. like
   c. admit
   d. be displeased about

2. Which homonym set was NOT used in the article?
   a. *knew* and *new*
   b. *threw* and *through*
   c. *died* and *dyed*
   d. *herd* and *heard*

3. What's the meaning of the homophone *real* as used in the article?
   a. actual
   b. rotation
   c. spindle
   d. roll

4. A homophone for *break* means
   a. crack.
   b. reduce speed.
   c. smash.
   d. accelerate.

5. Which of these words has a homograph that means "total"?
   a. live
   b. buffalo
   c. some
   d. bark

6. What does the homophone *sent* mean as used in the selection?
   a. moved
   b. one penny
   c. smell
   d. trace

PRACTICE 2: THE LAND DOWN UNDER

Read the selection, and then answer the questions that follow.

(1) Where do baby kangaroos come from? Australia, of course! That's *where* you'll find animal species <u>not</u> native to any other part of the world, like the koala, platypus, and kangaroo.

(2) Scientists say that about 600 million years ago, what we now *know* as Antarctica, South America, Africa, India, and Australia formed *one* huge continent called Gondwanaland. It was populated with dinosaurs and the first mammals—monotremes and marsupials. Monotremes, like the platypus, *lay* eggs from *which their* offspring hatch. Marsupials, like the kangaroo, *produce* offspring that develop *in* a pouch outside *their* mothers' bodies.

(3) Kangaroos are the largest marsupials. Males are called boomers, females *does*, and all babies are called joeys. What *does* the average kangaroo look like? Most adults are about 6 feet (1.8 m) tall and *weigh* about 100 pounds (45 kg). They have large hind feet, strong hind legs, and a *tail* measuring 3 feet (.9 m) or longer. A kangaroo uses its heavy tail for balance and *to* prop itself up when sitting or fighting, when it kicks the enemy with both hind feet! Normally kangaroos are quadrupeds—they use all *four* feet to walk. Even *their* short front limbs, like arms, help them move. *But* the animals stand on *two* feet when they want *to* move quickly. They can hop up to 40 miles (64 km) per *hour* over short distances and leap over 30 feet (9.2 m) *in* a single bound!

(4) About 130 million years ago, Gondwanaland broke apart and Australia was cut off from the rest of the world. Marsupials and monotremes still flourished *there*. *But* elsewhere, newer species of mammals appeared that gave birth to fully developed young. That's why you won't find kangaroos hopping across *present* day Antarctica!

7. As used in the article, which is the best meaning of the homograph *produce*?
   a. harvest
   b. bring into being
   c. give off
   d. foodstuffs

8. What is the meaning of the homophone *but* as used in the article?
   a. knock against
   b. strike
   c. end
   d. however

9. Which is a homophone for the underlined word in the third sentence?
   a. gnat
   b. knot
   c. graw
   d. know

10. Which of these words has a homograph that means "gift"?
    a. single
    b. balance
    c. present
    d. bound

11. Which homonym set was used in the article?
    a. *way* and *weigh*
    b. *four* and *for*
    c. *our* and *hour*
    d. *tail* and *tale*

12. Rewrite this sentence by replacing each underlined word with the correct homophone:

    What <u>wee</u> now <u>no</u> as Antarctica, South America, Africa, India, and Australia <u>awl</u> together formed <u>won</u> huge continent called Gondwanaland.

    _____

    _____

PRACTICE 3: WHAT CAN WE HEAR HERE?

Read this rhyme, and then answer the questions that follow.

> I went down by the *sea*, to find out what I could *see*,
> With *four* fine friends *for* company,
> We started down a *stair*, but all stopped to *stare*
> At a frog and a striped *bass* that we saw sitting *there*!
> The frog played a trumpet; the fish strummed a *bass*,
> And each of them had a big smile on his face!
> They finished *their* song, took a *bow* and turned to go,
> As a turtle gave them flowers all *tied* up with a *bow*!
> "Now what kind of *conduct* is this?" asked I,
> "To *conduct* a concert where people need to pass by?"
> "Oh, we only play *here* after the *tide* has come in,"
> Said the horn-playing frog with a large froggy grin.
> "Come up the *beach* now, over near that *beech* tree
> And you'll *hear* some jazz that's as cool as can be!"
> So we listened to their music and joined them in dance,
> You should really go hear them, if you have the chance!

13. The first homophone in line 3 means
    a. look at.
    b. step.
    c. rip apart.
    d. beach.

14. Which are NOT homophones?
    a. wear, where, ware
    b. by, buy, bye
    c. tide, tied, teid
    d. so, sew, sow

15. The homograph *bass* that rhymes with *face* means
    a. a kind of fish.
    b. a kind of beach.
    c. a kind of turtle.
    d. a musical instrument.

ANSWERS

1. d
2. c
3. a
4. b
5. c
6. a
7. b
8. d
9. b
10. c
11. b
12. What <u>we</u> now <u>know</u> as Antarctica, South America, Africa, India, and Australia <u>all</u> together formed <u>one</u> huge continent called Gondwanaland.
13. b
14. c
15. d

synonyms and antonyms

*A synonym is a word you use when you
can't spell the word you first thought of.*

BURT BACHARACH (1928–   )
AMERICAN PIANIST AND COMPOSER

In this lesson, you'll discover that two words may mean the same or mean just
the opposite.

KNOWING WORDS WITH the same or opposite meaning can help you make
sense of unknown words.

When you read, you may come across a word you don't know. You can
often figure out its meaning by thinking of a synonym or antonym for it.

A **synonym** means the same, or almost the same, as the unknown word.

Example
I felt so *ungainly*, tripping over my own feet as we headed to the dance
floor!

Can you think of a word to replace *ungainly* that would still describe someone
who trips? How about *clumsy*, *awkward*, or *gawky*? They all have about the
same meaning, but doesn't it sound more embarrassing to be *ungainly* than
clumsy? By using *ungainly*, the author tells you more about the person's feelings.

An **antonym** means the opposite of the unknown word.

Example

He collapsed after another *arduous* day of work in the mine.

Can you think of a word to describe work that probably would NOT make some-one collapse? How about *easy*, *simple*, or *effortless*? They all mean the opposite of *hard* or *difficult*, which is what *arduous* means!

Also, *or*, and *like* often signal a synonym is in the text near an unknown word. *But* or *unlike* often signal an antonym. Use the synonym or antonym to help you figure out the unknown word.

Example

Gigi thought she'd be calm once the test was over, but now she was *angst-ridden* about the results.

The word *but* in the example signals an antonym. Gigi thought she'd be calm, but she's the opposite. So *angst-ridden* must mean "anxious" or "worried."

Here are just a few words with their synonyms and antonyms. Note how a synonym may mean the same but give a different feeling to the original word.

Word	Synonym	Antonym
afraid	petrified	valiant
ask	interrogate	retort
begin	commence	terminate
correct	accurate	erroneous
friend	cohort	antagonist
laugh	chortle	snivel
naughty	mischievous	compliant
noisy	boisterous	tranquil
repair	renovate	demolish
small	minuscule	gargantuan
true	authentic	bogus

PRACTICE 1: PEBBLE POTTAGE

Based on a European Folktale

Read the selection, and then answer the questions that follow.

(1) One day, a *vagrant* knocked on a farmhouse door. The farmer's wife peered out at the weary *drifter*. "I can't let you in," she said, "for my husband is not at home. And besides, I have no *sustenance* to offer because my husband is bringing groceries back from town."

(2) "Then, Madam, you can share some of my pebble potage!" the man replied, and he pulled from his pocket what looked like an ordinary stone.

(3) "Pebble pottage?" asked the woman, suddenly interested in the ragged man.

(4) "Oh, yes, it is delicious," he said with a smile. "If I had a pot of water and a fire, I could demonstrate how this stone can magically make the best soup you've ever tasted!"

(5) The woman was curious, so she opened the door and the *wayfarer* came inside. Soon a pot of water was boiling away. He dropped in the stone, then tasted the watery broth. "It needs a pinch of salt, and a dash of pepper," he said. "You wouldn't have any, would you? And perhaps a tiny bit of butter?"

(6) "No problem," said the woman, and she ran to get the requested *components*.

(7) When she returned, he added the salt, pepper, and butter to the broth and tasted it again. "Yum. Much better!" he said. "But vegetables would add even more flavor! Are there none in your cellar or garden?"

(8) "Oh, there must be a few," she said, eager to taste the magic soup. So she ran to the garden and returned with some potatoes, carrots, and beans.

(9) These were added and the *vagabond* tasted the mixture again. "The magic stone has not failed me!" he whispered *surreptitiously*. "It is almost ready. All it needs is a bit of meat."

(10) The woman found some leftover chicken in the refrigerator and added it to the pot, saying, "Magic stone, do your thing!"

(11) Before long, a wonderful aroma filled the kitchen, *portending* that the soup was done. The woman filled a bowl for the man and one for herself. And there was enough left for her husband to have a bowlful when he returned.

(12) "Thank you so much for letting me use your pot and fire," the stranger said as he prepared to leave. He *extracted* his stone from the bottom of the pot, washed it off, and put it back into his pocket.

(13) "Oh, you are welcome. Do come again," said the woman.

(14) "Indeed I will," replied the hobo. "Now, because of your kindness, I want to leave you a gift." He fished into his other pocket and brought out a tiny pebble. "Here," he said with a smile, "is your very own magic pebble. It is not yet fully matured so it can only make enough soup for one. Use it well."

(15) Then he left and disappeared into the woods. The farmer's wife never saw him again, but she did enjoy a small cup of magic pebble pottage from time to time!

1. Which synonym was NOT used to describe the stranger?
   a. hobo
   b. vagrant
   c. wayfarer
   d. bum

2. An antonym for the word *extricated* is
   a. rescued.
   b. inserted.
   c. took out.
   d. removed.

3. Which is a synonym for *portending*?
   a. suggesting
   b. signifying
   c. indicating
   d. all of the above

4. Which is NOT an antonym for *surreptitiously*?
   a. sneakily
   b. furtively
   c. openly
   d. secretly

PRACTICE 2: HOT SPOT

Read the selection, and then answer the questions that follow.

(1)   The Panamint Indians, who were the *primary* inhabitants of California's Death Valley, called it *Tomesha*, meaning "ground afire." And it is a real hot spot. In fact, it holds the record for the highest temperature ever documented in the United States—134° F (57° C), recorded in July 1913! Death Valley also holds the record for the lowest point in the Western Hemisphere—a salty pool in Badwater, 282 feet (86 m) below sea level!

(2)   Normally, Death Valley gets only about 2 inches (5 cm) of rain annually. Some plants have adapted to the dry, desert life, as have kangaroo rats, scorpions, small lizards, and rattlesnakes. They find *sustenance* and can use the vegetation for shade in the extreme heat. But about every 50 years or so, it rains more in Death Valley. That's what happened in 2005. Winter storms dumped an *excessive* amount—6 inches (15 cm)—on the valley. The result? A rare showcase of color!

(3)   For decades, wildflower seeds with thick or waxy *veneers* had been germinating underground. When the heavy rains came, the additional moisture coaxed the seeds to bloom. And they did, in an array of beautiful color all over the desert floor!

(4)   The plants started a chain reaction. Caterpillars and moths flocked to the area to feed on the flowers. The insects then attracted birds and small rodents, which in turn attracted snakes and foxes, *fabricating* a whole new food chain in Death Valley.

(5)   Now the flowers are gone and the dry, hot weather has returned. But the blossoms dropped new seeds that will remain dormant in the ground waiting for the next really wet winter. Until then, other parts of the new food chain will have to look for nourishment elsewhere!

5. A synonym for the word *sustenance* is
  a. pollution.
  b. devastation.
  c. food.
  d. flooding.

6. Which in NOT an antonym for *fabricating*?
   a. constructing
   b. destroying
   c. devastating
   d. razing

7. The author could have used the synonym *sleeping* instead of
   a. array.
   b. vegetation.
   c. documented.
   d. dormant.

8. Which antonym pair is used in the selection?
   a. *tallest* and *shortest*
   b. *lowest* and *highest*
   c. *oldest* and *newest*
   d. *hottest* and *coldest*

9. Which is a synonym for *veneer*?
   a. roots
   b. veins
   c. stems
   d. coatings

10. A synonym for the word *excessive* is
   a. recessive.
   b. disproportionate.
   c. declined.
   d. meager.

PRACTICE 3: REVOLUTIONARY RESOLUTION

A Young Colonist's Decision

Read the poem, andthen answer the questions that follow.

> Patriot or Loyalist, which one will I be?
> My *kin* came here from England, but I'm a colonist, you see.
> We have *resided* here all of my life; we *toil* hard every day,
> So why should we pay *levies* to a *monarch* far away?
> The people who really love this land will *wrestle* to make it free.
> I love this land and I shall fight . . . so a Patriot I will be!
> Men and women, girls and boys, speak up for democracy,
> So we can *resolve* what's best for us, rather than someone across the sea!

11. Which is a synonym for *kin*?
- **a.** teacher
- **b.** family
- **c.** farmers
- **d.** engineer

12. If *resolve* means "choose," an antonym would be
- **a.** decide.
- **b.** determine.
- **c.** disallow.
- **d.** establish.

13. A synonym for *levies* is
- **a.** chairs.
- **b.** taxes.
- **c.** statues.
- **d.** attention.

14. An antonym for *toil* is
- **a.** relax.
- **b.** hustle.
- **c.** work.
- **d.** labor.

ANSWERS

1. d
2. b
3. d
4. c
5. c
6. a
7. d
8. b
9. d
10. b
11. b
12. c
13. b
14. a

4

prefixes and suffixes

My favorite letters are R and E; I add them
to turn so you'll come back to me!

GAYLE HOWARD (1945–   )
AMERICAN COUNTRY SINGER

In this lesson, you'll discover how word parts can help you figure out word meaning.

SOME WORDS ARE made up of parts, like base words, roots, prefixes, and suffixes.

A **base word** is a real word that can stand alone. You can make new words from it by adding other word parts.

Examples

Base word	Words made by adding parts
think	thinking, rethink, unthinkable, thinker
agree	agreeable, disagree, agreement

A **root** can't stand alone. Many roots come from Greek or Latin words.

Examples

Root	Origin	English example
dict	Latin for *say*	diction
spect	Greek for *observe*	inspect

A **prefix** is a group of letters added to the beginning of a base word, like the *re-* in *rethink*. A prefix changes the meaning of the base word.

Examples

Prefix	Meaning	Example
sub	under	submarine, underwater vessel
un-	not	unbelieveable, not to be believed

A **suffix** is a group of letters added to the end of a base word. The suffix also changes the meaning of the base word.

Examples

Suffix	Meaning	Examples
-less	without	sleepless, clueless, hopeless
-ly	in that way	gladly, quickly, immediately

You can use word parts to help you figure out the meaning of unknown words. Look at parts of the word. Do you recognize the base word? Be aware that added parts can change the base word's part of speech. For example, a verb might become a noun or a noun might become an adjective. Put the parts together and guess the meaning. Try out your idea in the sentence. If it makes sense, you're most likely right!

Example

I know he was upset, but his actions were *indefensible*!

Prefix	Base	Suffix
in-	defens	-ible
not-	justif(justify)	-able

Put the parts together: not *justifiable*. Try it in the sentence: I know he was upset, but his actions were not *justifiable*! Does it make sense? Yes!

PRACTICE 1: THE BIRD WOMAN

Read the selection, and then answer the questions that follow.

(1)   In 1804, explorers Meriwether Lewis and William Clark set out on an expedition to map thousands of miles, from the Dakotas to the Pacific Ocean. They knew they needed horses to cross the mountains, and that the

Shoshone in the territory had horses. But Lewis and Clark didn't speak the Shoshone language, so how would they be able to trade with the Shoshone for fresh horses? Happily, the explorers found a solution. They would take along Sacagawea, a Shoshone whose name means "Bird Woman," to speak for them.

(2)   On the long journey, Sacagawea did more than just intervene with the Shoshone for the explorers. She also helped the group survive. She could predict which plants were safe to eat and prepared nutritious meals. She used natural materials to make clothing for them to wear and medicines to cure their ills. And she reassured other Indian tribes along the way that the explorers were on a peaceful mission and meant them no harm. Just the sight of a young woman, who also brought along her young child, convinced tribes that this was no war party.

(3)   Sacagawea also showed her bravery. When a sudden gust of strong wind almost capsized the boat in which she was riding, Sacagawea remained calm. She carefully recovered many important papers, medicine, and other vital supplies that would otherwise have been lost. Sacagawea's calmness under pressure and her hard work, earned high praise from Lewis and Clark. They honored her by naming part of a Montana river "Bird Woman's River." Later, statues of Sacagawea and books about her kept her memory alive. And in 2000, the U.S. Mint even honored Sacagawea by putting her image on a gold dollar coin!

1. The root *dict* means "say" and the prefix *pre-* means "before," so *predict* means
   a. say afterwards, or contradict.
   b. tell again, or repeat.
   c. refuse to say, deny.
   d. say in advance, or foretell.

2. What does *happily* mean?
   a. happy again
   b. happy together
   c. in a happy way
   d. not in a good mood

3. The *peace* in *peaceful* is
   a. a root word.
   b. a base word.
   c. a prefix.
   d. a suffix.

4. The prefix *re-* means "again," so the word *reassured* means
   a. guaranteed again.
   b. forgot again.
   c. gave a gift again.
   d. all of the above

5. Which is the meaning of *calmness*?
   a. to be stressed again
   b. having an advantage
   c. the state of being calm
   d. have a reason to worry

6. How would knowing the root *ven* means "come, go" and the prefix *inter-* means "between" help you figure out the meaning of *intervene* as used in the selection?

_____

_____

PRACTICE 2: PAWS FOR ALARM

Read the selection, and then answer the questions that follow.

(1) It was late when Dad pulled the van up to the old ski cabin. I grabbed a suitcase and headed toward the front door. My cat Sage jumped out to follow me, daintily scampering to keep the cold, wet snow away from her paws. Sage had a touch of arthritis and didn't find winter weather enjoyable!

(2) A sizeable carpet of snow covered the porch, so I dragged my feet to make a path for us. Dad unlocked the door and Sage scurried inside, looking for a dry place to nap. Dad built a fire in the old fireplace, and soon the room was warm and cozy.

(3) I went down the hall to my room, with Sage behind me. She jumped up on my bed and curled up in a small furry ball. "I'll be joining you soon," I said.

(4) Just then, Dad popped his head into the room. "Let's call it a day," he said with a yawn. "See you in the morning for an early ski?"

(5) I nodded in agreement, and Dad went to his room and shut the door. As I slipped under the covers, I looked out the window at the snow falling ever faster. "The ski runs will be awesome tomorrow!" I mumbled sleepily.

(6) I don't know how long I was asleep before Sage's whiskers rubbed against my face. "Stop," I pleaded gently, but she purred loudly and pushed me with her head. "Stop!" I hissed, not even opening my eyes. She let out a loud MEOW! This was so unlike her. She'd slept beside me since she was a kitten, and she'd never bothered me before! Just as I was about to drift back into a peaceful sleep, she leaped on me with all four paws . . . HARD! Then she zipped across the room and slammed up against the window glass! THUMP!

(7) I opened my eyes, but everything was foggy . . . and my head hurt. Then I coughed . . . smoke . . . there was smoke seeping in under the door! I didn't open the door, I felt it like firefighters say you should. The wood was hot . . . that meant there was fire on the other side! We had to get out!

(8) Sage batted her paws against the window glass. "Okay, I get it," I cried as I ran to open the window, but it was stuck! I continued to push, and at last, it opened. Cold, fresh air filled my lungs as we climbed out the window. I picked up Sage and ran to the window of Dad's room. I banged on the glass, but he didn't answer. So I threw a rock to break the glass, and screamed his name. Finally, he stumbled to the window and scrambled out.

(9) The firefighters who put out the blaze said sparks from the fireplace had set the rug on fire. "We'll put in smoke alarms today," Dad said. "I only wish we'd had them last night!"

(10) "From what I hear, you had a live smoke alarm," one firefighter said, stroking Sage's soft fur. "She's quite a hero!" Sage just purred and closed her eyes, anxious to get that nap at last!

7. If the root *artho* means "joint" and the suffix *-itis* means "inflammation," Sage most likely
   a. has difficulty hearing.
   b. has aches and pains in her legs.
   c. has difficulty seeing.
   d. has a problem eating cat food.

8. The suffix *-able* means "capable of being" and changes the base word *size*
   a. to a pronoun.
   b. to a verb.
   c. to an adjective.
   d. to a plural noun.

9. The prefix *un-* changes the base word *like* to mean
   a. the same.
   b. not understood.
   c. not known.
   d. not similar.

10. If the prefix *ad-* means "to" and the Latin word *jacere* means "lie near," the word *adjacent* means
   a. far-off.
   b. adjoining.
   c. distant.
   d. none of the above

PRACTICE 3: FURRY FORECASTER

Read the selection, and then answer the questions that follow.

(1)   February 2 is Groundhog Day. In many places, people believe that on that day, the groundhog will come out of its subterranean burrow and predict the weather. Legends say that if it's sunny that day, the groundhog will see its shadow, be frightened, go back into its burrow, and sleep some more. This is supposed to indicate that spring is still six weeks away.

(2)   The legends add that if it's cloudy, the groundhog won't see a shadow, so it will remain above ground. This is supposed to be a sign that spring will soon arrive! So every February, reporters rush to witness a groundhog pop up from underground. The journalists write about what happens and TV shows air video of the action as the groundhog exits its winter home.

(3)   Are the legends believable? Well, scientists have recorded that clear February days are often followed by much colder ones. And it's been noted that cloudy days in February are usually warm. Historical weather documents reveal that sometimes the groundhog is right, but other times it is mistaken. If you really want to know what the weather will be, check your local TV meteorologist!

11. Since *terra* means "Earth," *subterranean* means
   a. above ground.
   b. below ground.
   c. at ground level.
   d. over the ground.

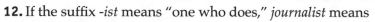

12. If the suffix *-ist* means "one who does," *journalist* means
   a. a person who sings.
   b. a person who cooks.
   c. a person who writes.
   d. a person who builds.

13. Which is the meaning of *believable* as used in the article?
   a. able to organize
   b. not truthful
   c. suspected
   d. worthy of belief

ANSWERS

   1. d
   2. c
   3. b
   4. a
   5. c
   6. Knowing that *ven* means "come, go" and *inter-* means "between" helps me know that *intervene* means someone's a go-between, getting both sides to agree on something.
   7. b
   8. c
   9. d
   10. b
   11. b
   12. c
   13. d

5

terminology and jargon

It is more fun to talk with someone who doesn't use long, difficult words but rather short, easy words like "What about lunch?"

A. A. MILNE (1882–1956)
ENGLISH AUTHOR "WINNIE THE POOH"

In this lesson, you'll discover that the words you use may differ, depending on who you're talking to.

PEOPLE WHO WORK together or do things as a group may have their own language of special terms, or jargon, that makes it easy for them to communicate with one another. For example, if you use the Internet, you know what IM (instant message), website, and sayings like LOL (laugh out loud) mean. But someone who's never used a computer might be very confused! There are special terms and jargon that relate to science, art, music, cooking, politics, and just about any topic. On the following page are some examples.

Word	Topic	Meaning
aperture	photography	camera lens opening
apogee	space	an orbiting object's highest point from Earth
blog	Internet	short for Weblog, a personal journal to share online
braise	cooking	prepare slowly with little moisture in a closed pot
caucus	politics	a meeting of only members in a political party
colonnade	architecture	row of columns
currency	banking	coins and paper money
ligaments	medicine	fibers that connect bones
subtrahend	math	number that is to be subtracted
wings	theater	areas off both sides of the main stage

Read this sample of jargon and see if you can guess what group of people might use the language.

> Squeeze one, two chicks on a raft—wreck 'em, shingle with a shimmy and a shake, and city juice—86 the hail.

If you guessed people who work in a restaurant, especially a diner, you're right. It's how some waiters give an order for one orange juice, two eggs on toast—scrambled, buttered toast with jam, and water—hold the ice! Now that's really a special vocabulary.

PRACTICE 1: QUIET ON THE SET!

Read the selection, and then answer the questions that follow.

(1) Last summer I visited my uncle Ron. The public relations firm he works for was handling the ads for an upcoming movie, and he took me to watch a shoot! "Let's go meet the a.d.," Ron said when we got to the studio.

(2) "You *meet* an ad?" I asked, a little confused.

(3) "Oh, sorry, that's the assistant director," he laughed. "You get so used to the jargon on the set that you figure everyone else knows it."

(4) The a.d., whose name was Mim, pointed out that "The d.p. is using a dolly to track some actors running a scene." I guess I looked confused because she smiled, "He's the director of photography, or cinematographer . . . around here we just call him the d.p. He runs the camera; it's his job to get the best shot every time!"

(5) "And the camera's on a dolly," I said knowingly, "I saw a platform on wheels like that at my dad's store. It's on tracks, like a train. Is it always there?"

(6) "No, we move them after the d.p. gets the final shot," she replied.

(7) Just then, someone called, "Where's the gaffer? We need a blue gel. And can someone just close the barn door on that one?" he called, pointing up.

(8) "They need an electrician," Uncle Ron whispered. "They want a blue filter over the light . . . blue light is softer, not so harsh."

(9) "Got it," I replied. "But what's a barn door?"

(10) Mim pointed up at the huge lights. "See the flaps on the front of the light? They can be opened or closed to give more or less light. We call them barn doors."

(11) I didn't say it, but I thought, "That's silly; why not just call them flaps?"

(12) Later, I saw two actors filming a sword fight in front of a green wall. "Without scenery, how will anyone know if they're in a castle or on a cliff?" I asked.

(13) "That's where c.g.i. comes in," explained Mim. "The action is filmed in front of a blue or green screen, then a computer-generated image is dropped in for the background. It'll make them look like they're dueling atop the Statue of Liberty or in a hall at Buckingham Palace, whatever the filmmakers want."

(14) "So if I see an actor riding a camel in a desert, is he really doing it?" I asked.

(15) "Sometimes," Mim replied. "Some films are shot on location at different spots around the world. But it costs less to use blue-screen and c.g.i., so it's up to the filmmakers and their budget. They may want *movie magic*."

(16) "We need background people for the next scene," someone called to Mim.

(17) She nodded. "Time for me to make sure the people you may know as *extras* are in place," she confided. "They're the ones who give the scene a sense of reality—folks walking down a street or shopping in a mall as the stars do their thing."

(18)   After lunch, we watched more filming. "Quiet on the set!" someone called. "Rolling! Action!"

(19)   The background people began to move, then into the scene rode the hero, the star of the movie, on a real motorcycle! No green screen needed!

1. In which would you most likely use jargon like *cinematographer*?
   a. medicine
   b. sports
   c. construction
   d. film production

2. What is the meaning of *a.d.* as used in the selection?
   a. after delivery
   b. artistic director
   c. assistant director
   d. actors' directory

3. A gaffer is
   a. in charge of serving lunch on a movie set.
   b. a worker for an advertising agency.
   c. the star of a movie.
   d. an electrician.

4. A c.g.i. is dropped in as background for action that's shot in front of
   a. a live audience.
   b. a blue or green screen.
   c. Buckingham Palace.
   d. a white screen.

PRACTICE 2: MONEY MATTERS

Read the selection, and then answer the questions that follow.

(1)   Today we use two basic kinds of currency, or money: metal coins and paper bills. But once people bartered, or traded, for things they needed or wanted. In ancient Africa, salt was really valuable because people in many places didn't have it, and they needed it to flavor and preserve their food. So people would trade a bag of gold for a bag of salt!

(2)   Then, about 3,500 years ago, people started using seashells as money. The North American Indians used wampum, beads made of clamshells. In about 1,000 B.C., the Chinese minted the first metal coins. They had holes in the centers so they could be carried on a string, kind of like a key ring. Later, the Chinese invented paper money.

(3)   Before long, people around the world used coins and paper money to buy goods. Most people kept their money at home, tucked under a mattress or a floorboard, or stuffed in a jar. But often the money was stolen or lost in a flood or fire. And sometimes people just forgot where they had hidden it! That's why banks were built. The special buildings were equipped with vaults—rooms where everyone's money was locked up and guarded. People who put their money in a bank felt that the cash was safe.

(4)   The first bank in the United States opened in 1791. Today there are thousands. To open an account at a bank, a person must be at least 18 years old. That's because only adults can legally sign papers needed to open the account. An account holder can deposit, or put in, more money from time to time. It's added to the balance, or total already in the account. He or she can also withdraw, or take out, money that's then subtracted from the balance.

(5)   People can deposit or withdraw money at the bank or at an ATM (Automatic Teller Machine). Each account holder is given a plastic card that electronically holds information about the account. The machine scans the card, then allows the person to deposit or withdraw money, or check the current balance.

5. Jargon like *currency*, *deposit*, and *ATM* are used in the field of
   a. baking.
   b. science
   c. banking.
   d. auto racing.

6. What is the meaning of *mint* as used in the selection?
   a. a flavored candy
   b. flawless
   c. green, leafy plant
   d. produced

7. What is the meaning of *vault* as used in the selection?
  a. to leap over
  b. a burial chamber
  c. a room for the safekeeping of valuables
  d. to cover

8. Wampum was currency made from
  a. clamshells.
  b. turkey feathers.
  c. salt.
  d. paper.

9. To open a bank account, a person must be
  a. an American citizen.
  b. at least 18 years old.
  c. at least 21 years old.
  d. a high school graduate.

10. The meaning of *balance* as used in the selection is
  a. steadiness.
  b. set of scales.
  c. total.
  d. compare.

PRACTICE 3: MANAGE MINERALS

Read the selection, and then answer the questions that follow.

(1)   Rocks are made of minerals. Those are substances that can't be classified as "animals" or "vegetables." There are many different minerals. Each can be identified by its properties, or characteristics. To identify a mineral, scientists test its streak, hardness, luster, color, and cleavage.

(2)   To test the streak, the mineral is rubbed on a marble slab to see if it leaves a mark, and if so, what color mark. To test hardness, the mineral is scratched on glass to see if it scratches the glass, and if so, how much. Scientists can see the mineral's luster, or shininess, to know if it's metallic or nonmetallic. The mineral's color is also obvious to the eye. Finally, the mineral is checked for cleavage—breaks, or fractures, along weak points.

(3)   An accurate identification of a mineral can't be done by checking just one property. Many minerals have similar properties, such as the same hardness or color. Always test all the properties before stating for sure which mineral it is.

11. In which topic would you most likely find words like *minerals* and *metallic*?
   a. music
   b. cooking
   c. science
   d. ballet

12. Every substance is classified as either an animal, a vegetable, or a
   a. mineral.
   b. human.
   c. solid.
   d. liquid.

13. What is the meaning of *streak* as used in the article?
   a. run fast
   b. a mark of color
   c. to distort
   d. to stretch

ANSWERS

   1. d
   2. c
   3. d
   4. b
   5. c
   6. d
   7. c
   8. a
   9. b
   10. c
   11. c
   12. a
   13. b

LESSON 6

context clues

If I could tell you what it meant,
there would be no point in dancing it.

ISADORA DUNCAN (1877–1927)
AMERICAN, ONE OF THE FOUNDERS OF MODERN DANCE

In this lesson, you'll discover that authors give clues in the text to help you understand what you read. You just have to be a word detective and find them!

SOMETIMES AUTHORS NEED or want to use words they know will be
unknown by their readers. So authors slip in other words or phrases to help
readers figure out the unknown ones. Authors may define the word, give examples of similar things, or restate the idea to make it clearer. And authors may put
the clues in the text itself or in nearby pictures. Readers use these context clues
to make good guesses about what unknown words mean.

Definition
He played the *harpsichord*, a piano-like musical instrument.

Examples
The largest group is *arthropods*, like spiders, insects, and lobsters.

Restate to clarify
She ran to the *escarpment*. Could she climb down the steep hill in time to
escape?

Sometimes an author just wants readers to understand the context of a
word, not necessarily the exact meaning.

Dan was surprised that he hadn't won the election. "That's *implausible!*" he whined.

Now you may not know exactly what *implausible* means, but you can get the idea that it's not good because Dan whines, so he's not *happily* surprised! (**Implausible** means *unbelievable*.)

Look for all kinds of context clues to help you as you read.

PRACTICE 1: PLANNING AHEAD

Read the selection, and then answer the questions that follow.

(1) It was late when Marco finally got to the store. He'd been planning this surprise party for weeks, but somehow time was running out! "I can handle it all by myself," he'd told his mom when he first suggested a surprise party for his cousin's birthday. "I mean, how hard it is to throw a party?"

(2) "It can be very time-consuming. There's a lot to do," replied his mom. But Marco reiterated, "I can handle it all myself!"

(3) Marco did all the mundane, tedious things first, like making a list of who to invite, buying the invitations, and addressing and mailing them out. He found it somewhat irritating when people called to RSVP right in the middle of his favorite TV show, but he thanked them and checked their names on the list so he'd know who would and wouldn't be attending the party.

(4) Then he planned the menu. He knew Paco loved Crema Catalana—a cold custard with a crispy, crunchy, caramel coating. Marco thought his mom made the best, so he asked her to make it for the party. Of course, he planned to have a giant birthday cake with candles for Paco to blow out for luck. Marco also picked other good things to serve.

(5) The day of the party, Marco blew up balloons and made colorful garlands. He draped the paper-chain ribbons across the curtains and attached the balloons to the wall with double-stick tape. Everything looked quite festive. He called his Uncle Santiago to make sure he'd bring Paco at the right time, supposedly just to drop in for a minute on the way to dinner. Then Marco checked on the food supplies. The snacks were ready. The Crema Catalana was in the refrigerator keeping cold, awaiting that final, last-minute caramel topping. And the cake was ready, awaiting the candles on top. . . . "Oh, no!" Marco cried. "I forgot to pick up candles! Mom, do we have any birthday candles?"

(6) "Sorry, honey," she replied. "I wish you'd told me. . . . I could have picked some up on the way home. You'll have to run to the store to get some."

(7) And that's how Marco ended up at the store just before closing, when there was just one checkout open, and a very slow clerk. The lady in front of Marco kept asking, "Is it always this slow?" After the fifth time, Marco replied, somewhat politely, "Yes, ma'am, except on Thursdays. Why don't you come back then?"

(8) The lady turned in a huff and galumphed out of the store, leaving one less person in front of Marco.

(9) Finally, Marco got to the counter. "I just have these birthday candles, Ma'am, and I can't be late for the party," he said hurriedly as he put some money on the counter. "Just keep the change!"

(10) He ran home as fast as he could, arriving just in time to hear everyone inside yell "Surprise!" as Paco and Uncle Santiago walked in the door ahead of him!

1. Which is most likely the meaning of *reiterate*?
   a. refused
   b. said for the first time
   c. said again
   d. sat down

2. Which is NOT a meaning of *mundane*?
   a. boring
   b. ordinary
   c. dull
   d. unusual

3. What kind of context clue does the author use for Crema Catalana?
   a. an example of a similar dessert
   b. a definition
   c. a synonym
   d. none of the above

4. What kind of context clue does the author use for *garlands*?
   a. a definition
   b. an antonym
   c. a restatement to clarify
   d. examples of other hanging objects

5. From the context, which is most likely the meaning of *galumphed*?
   a. tip-toed
   b. ran
   c. stomped
   d. skipped

PRACTICE 2: IN SIGHT

Read the selection, and then answer the questions that follow.

(1) What causes myopia? You probably know that we see because light bounces off objects and into our eyes. In a normal eye, the light rays go through the lens and focus on the retina, the sensory membrane or sheet that lines the eye, to create images. In myopic eyes, the light focuses in front of the retina instead of directly on it. So nearsighted people can usually see really well up close, but they squint to try to see things far away.

(2) Often, nearsightedness is suspected if a kid has trouble seeing the chalk-board or whiteboard in school. Then a vision test is set up to diagnose perception. In other words, a doctor checks how well the person can read various sized letters at various distances.

(3) Early diagnosis is important because nearsightedness can be ameliorated with corrective visual devices, like glasses and contact lenses. These devices can't "cure" myopia, but they help a nearsighted person see distant objects more clearly. The lens of the glasses or contacts refocuses the light before it reaches the eye so it hits the retina where it should.

(4) Doctors can also do surgery to help some people who have myopia. Adults with myopia, whose glasses or contact prescription hasn't changed for at least a year, may be able to have a laser procedure that can clear up their problem.

(5) Nearsightedness affects men and women equally. People with a family history of myopia are more likely to develop it. And there's no way to prevent it. At one time people actually believed that reading too much or watching too much TV caused nearsightedness. Those activities can make your eyes tired, but they can't cause myopia.

6. What kind of context clue does the author use for *myopia*?
  a. a restatement to clarify
  b. a definition
  c. a homonym
  d. examples of other eye problems

7. What is the retina?
  a. a ray of light
  b. a lens
  c. a membrane, or lining
  d. a light shaft

8. What is the meaning of *diagnose*?
  a. detect
  b. identify
  c. analyze
  d. all of the above

9. Which is most likely the meaning of *ameliorated*?
  a. worsened
  b. improved
  c. continued
  d. renewed

10. For which does the author give two or more examples as context clues?
  a. kinds of membranes in the body
  b. lenses in cameras
  c. corrective visual devices
  d. types of eye conditions

11. If you didn't know the meaning of *surgery*, which nearby word would be a clue?
  a. doctors
  b. myopia
  c. glasses
  d. problem

PRACTICE 2: VAST VESSELS

Read the selection, and then answer the questions that follow.

(1)   Galleons were large ships used by Europeans from the sixteenth to eighteenth centuries. Equipped with three or four masts and two or more decks, these gallant ships helped countries like Spain and England establish their naval power.

(2)   A galleon's sides were 3–4 feet (.9–1.2 m) thick, strong enough to hold the heavy foremast and mainmast, both equipped with huge square sails. The foremast was, as the word *fore* suggests, the one closest to the front, or bow, of the ship. One or two smaller masts were toward the ship's stern, or rear. They had lateens—three-cornered sails. Openings on the ship's sides held heavy cannons.

(3)   After the discovery of the Americas, the Spanish used fleets of galleons to ship home chattel from the Americas, like gold, silver, and precious gems. But many ships never made it back. Hard to maneuver, they often couldn't evade lighter pirate ships. And many galleons sank during violent hurricanes. Today, treasure-hunting divers still find the wreckage of the majestic ships and their caches of riches today.

12. A foremast is
    a. the mast closest to the stern.
    b. the mast closest to the bow.
    c. the mast in the middle.
    d. the tallest mast.

13. Which is most likely the meaning of *chattel*?
    a. lands
    b. information
    c. advice
    d. possessions

14. From the context of the selection, *maneuver* most likely means
    a. study or read
    b. paint and restore.
    c. steer or guide.
    d. submerge and sink.

ANSWERS

1. a
2. d
3. b
4. a
5. c
6. b
7. c
8. d
9. b
10. c
11. a
12. b
13. d
14. c

7

denotation and connotation

*The name "reservation" has a negative connotation among
Native Americans—an intern camp of sorts.*
JOHN RUSSELL (1921–1991)
AMERICAN ACTOR

In this lesson, you'll find that a word may suggest something quite different from what it really means.

EVERY WORD HAS a denotation—its definition as found in a dictionary. But many words also have a connotation—the feelings or images they bring to mind.

Example
snake
Denotation: scaly, legless reptile
Connotation: danger, evil, disloyal person

Even words that mean the same may have different connotations. Think about the synonyms *scary* and *terrifying*. They have similar meanings, but produce different feelings. There's a big difference between the scary sound of the howling wind and a terrifying experience like falling off a cliff!

Authors choose words to influence how readers feel. The words may suggest positive or negative connotations.

Example

I saw many *homeless people* on the streets of the city. *(positive)*

I saw many *bums* on the streets of the city. *(negative)*

Here are a few more positive and negative connotations of words.

Word Use	Positive	Negative
Grandpa is *thrifty*.	spends money wisely	cheap
She's very *strong-willed*.	determined	stubborn
He has good *self-esteem*.	proud of work well done	conceited
She was tall and *slender*.	slim	anorexic
He's an *eager* leader.	enthusiastic	impatient

As you read, look for both positive and negative connotations. Ask yourself why the author wants you to get that connotation.

PRACTICE 1: "IT'S FOR YOU!"

Read the selection, and then answer the questions that follow.

(1)   You can't go anywhere today without running into someone using a cell phone. People are either talking on them or texting. Okay, so we know the handheld devices are helpful tools, but shouldn't there be some rules about their use in society? Just because someone has a cell phone, does that make it okay to talk rowdily on it in public? Does everyone in the vicinity have to be bombarded with one-sided conversations, even if they don't want to? Not everyone agrees.

(2)   Some people, usually those who use their cells a lot, say it's totally okay to use them anywhere, anytime. They may allege, "America's a free country and it's my right to talk in public! Other people talk to each other all the time while they walk down the street or eat in a restaurant. What's the difference if I talk to someone face-to-face or on a cell? If other people don't like hearing my phone conversations, they don't have to listen! I think *they* should move away from me so they don't hear what I'm saying! After all, it's very rude to eavesdrop! Besides, cells phones are essential in today's world. You see stories on TV all the time about people trapped in elevators, or under rubble from earthquakes or hurricanes, who used their cells to get help that saved their lives. And cells help kids keep in touch with their families . . . so the kids and their parents feel safer!"

(3)   Other people see things differently and say things like, "Public places are for everyone. It's true that this is a free country, so why should I be forced to listen to loud talking and laughing, especially when it's usually about stuff that's really lame or should be private anyway? Trust me, no one wants to hear about the fight you had with your friend, the movie you saw, or what you're wearing to the school dance! People should be able to hang out at the mall or ride a bus without hearing brainless conversations. Last week I was almost knocked down by someone skating at the ice rink and talking on the phone at the same time! If it's important enough for you to call someone, take the time to do it right. A phone conversation is private, so keep yours to yourself! Talking on a cell in public is not only bad-mannered, it adds to noise pollution!"

(4)   Is there a happy medium between using a cell "wherever and whenever" and outlawing its use altogether? Sure, it's called common sense. Be respectful of other people's rights. Don't talk so loudly on the phone. . . . The person on the other end can hear just fine without your shouting . . . and adjust the ring tones so you don't hog the air that's for all to share.

1. Which word could the author have used instead of *rowdily* that means the same but has a less negative connotation?
   a. softly
   b. loudly
   c. happily
   d. quietly

2. Which word in the following sentence gives a negative connotation?
   They may allege, "America's a free country and it's my right to talk in public!"
   a. free
   b. right
   c. allege
   d. public

3. Which word in the second paragraph is a positive connotation for *important*?
   a. essential
   b. difference
   c. conversation
   d. eavesdrop

4. What is the denotation of the word *hog*? What is its connotation in the last paragraph? Why do you think the author used that word?

_____

_____

_____

PRACTICE 2: ONLY WOMAN MEDAL OF HONOR WINNER

Read the selection, and then answer the questions that follow.

(1)   As a child, they say Mary Walker was a bit of a brat. She always wanted to do things differently. When she grew up, she continued to do so, becoming the first woman military doctor, a prisoner of war, a spy, and the only woman to win the Medal of Honor, America's highest military award.

(2)   Born in 1832, Walker graduated from medical school at the age of 21. She was the only female in her class and only the second U.S. woman to graduate from a medical school. When the Civil War broke out, she went to Washington, D.C. to become an Army surgeon. The Army gave her a tough time, so she volunteered as a nurse and went off to treat wounded soldiers.

(3)   The Army finally conceded and appointed her as an assistant surgeon in 1863, making her the first female doctor in the U.S. Army. The foxy Walker designed a military uniform for herself—a knee-length skirt over trousers and a man's uniform jacket. To those unhappy with her garb, she clarified that the hoop skirts women normally wore were too cumbersome and dangerous when she was working in field hospitals and on battlefields.

(4)   As a dedicated doctor, Walker treated those in need, no matter what their politics. So she often crossed Confederate lines to treat civilians. It's generally accepted that while in enemy territory, she was also working as a spy for the North. On one of these trips, she was captured by Confederate troops and held in a Southern prison until both sides exchanged captives.

(5)   The Army nominated Walker for the Medal of Honor and she was awarded it in 1866. Her citation praises her wartime service but doesn't specifically mention valor in combat. That turned out to be an important oversight.

(6) In 1916, the government began reviewing Medal of Honor awards. Over the years, the medal had been copied and sold, and many people wore medals illegally. Congress revised the standard for awarding a Medal of Honor to mandate it only be given for actual combat with an enemy.

(7) Mary Walker and hundreds of past Medal of Honor recipients were stripped of their medals. The government demanded Walker and the others return theirs. She refused and wore hers until her death at age 87 in 1919.

(8) In the late 1960s, Mary's great-grandniece launched a campaign to restore the medal her great-aunt had earned. Congress studied the case, and in 1977, President Jimmy Carter reinstated Mary Walker's Medal of Honor.

5. A denotation of *foxy* is "like a fox" and the connotation is
   a. dull.
   b. clever.
   c. bashful.
   d. frightened.

6. Which word gives a negative connotation to doing things differently?
   a. continued
   b. graduated
   c. brat
   d. child

7. Which is probably the most positive connotation of *conceded*?
   a. okayed
   b. contracted
   c. denied
   d. tolerated

8. Which connotation is most negative?
   a. prisoner
   b. detainee
   c. hostage
   d. inmate

9. "... stripped of their medals" gives a more negative connotation to
   a. exchanging prisoners of war.
   b. working in a field hospital.
   c. requesting a commission as an army surgeon.
   d. taking away an award.

10. Which word that means the same as *demanded* is more positive?
   a. commanded
   b. asked
   c. decreed
   d. required

PRACTICE 3: WHY THE GIRAFFE'S NECK IS LONG

Read the selection, and then answer the questions that follow.

(1)   Once giraffes had short necks, like horses. The giraffes ate grass, bushes, and leaves near the bottoms of trees. But the greedy animals ate and ate until all the plants were gone, except for the leaves at the very tops of the tallest trees. To get them, the giraffes stood on one another's heads! It was quite uncomfortable, to say the least, but the leaves were tender and juicy.

(2)   One day, Gayle Giraffe was perched on top, nibbling away at the leaves. Suddenly, the giraffes under her moved away, leaving her head stuck between two branches! There she dangled, far above the ground. The clever giraffe didn't panic; she took a deep breath and stretched her body agonizingly until her hoofs felt the soft earth. Then, she pulled her neck free.

(3)   "Look!" said another giraffe, who had witnessed the struggle. "Gayle's neck has stretched! Now she can reach the leaves without climbing!"

(4)   So one by one, the others stuck their heads into the branches and stretched their necks. A few giraffes were chicken and didn't want to do it, but they finally did. And now, all giraffes can eat the juiciest leaves in the treetops any time!

11. Which word could the author have used instead of *greedy* that means the same thing but does NOT have a negative connotation?
  a. miserly
  b. gluttonous
  c. selfish
  d. hungry

12. A denotation of *chicken* is "a barnyard fowl" and the connotation is
  a. "a brave person."
  b. "a squawking person."
  c. "a coward."
  d. "a clown."

13. Which of these words from the story has a positive connotation?
  a. agonizingly
  b. clever
  c. dangled
  d. panic

ANSWERS

  1. b
  2. c
  3. a
  4. A hog is a large pig. The connotation is someone who takes more than a fair share or is selfish. The author probably used the word to stress that he or she believes some cell phone users don't respect the rights of others.
  5. b
  6. c
  7. a
  8. c
  9. d
  10. b
  11. d
  12. c
  13. b

SECTION 2

variety in reading

WHAT'S TO READ?

Everywhere you look, you find something to read. Maybe it's an ad on the back of a cereal box. Maybe it's an article in a newspaper or magazine. Maybe it's a school textbook. Maybe it's a bus schedule. Or maybe it's a sign on a store window that says CLOSED when you want to buy something! Our lives are filled with words to read, but we may need different kinds of skills to read and comprehend different kinds of writing. In this section of the book, you'll learn how to

- distinguish between genres of fiction and nonfiction.
- identify an author's purpose for writing.
- analyze an author's style and tone.
- recognize text features and how authors use them.
- examine an author's use of graphics.

genre: fiction or nonfiction?

The difference between fiction and reality?
Fiction has to make sense.

TOM CLANCY (1947–   )
AMERICAN WRITER OF POLITICAL THRILLER

In this lesson, you'll learn that some stories are true and some are made up by writers!

FICTION IS A story an author makes up.

Nonfiction is information based on facts about the real world. Here are some ways you can tell the difference.

Fiction	Nonfiction
has at least one character	may or may not have characters
characters may or may not be real and may or may not be human	any character is or was alive, often uses dates and statistics
has a story: a plot or series of events	may or may not have a story
may be about real or imaginary places and events	always about real places or events, tells dates when events happened

Sometimes, fiction may seem like nonfiction because the author writes about people, places, or events that you know are real.

Example
The astronaut left the life capsule and followed the slimy tracks across the surface of Mars.

Example

Did you ever wonder if there really could be life on Mars? Yesterday, scientists at NASA sent a space probe to find out.

Genre is a word that means "kind" or "variety." There are many different genres of fiction and nonfiction. Here's how to identify a few.

Genre	Fiction/ Nonfiction	Identifying Elements
autobiography	nonfiction	story about a person's life written by that person
biography	nonfiction	story about a person's life written by someone else
blog	nonfiction	personal journal on the Internet
encyclopedia	nonfiction	facts and statistics about people, places, and things
fable	fiction	old story that teaches a moral, or lesson
fairytale	fiction	story about make-believe beings and events
folktale	fiction	story passed from generation to generation
journal	nonfiction	personal stories about events in real life
legend	fiction	larger-than-life story told as if it were true
magazine	nonfiction	articles, stories, and other features
mystery	nonfiction	story about unexplained happenings
myth	fiction	very old story that "explains" something in nature
newspaper	nonfiction	facts about what's happening in the world
novel	fiction	long story, usually in chapters
play	fiction	dialogue and directions for actors, scenes, and acts
poetry	fiction	has rhythm, may rhyme, may have stanzas (sections)
science fiction	fiction	story about effects of science on society
short story	fiction	can be read in one session
textbook	nonfiction	information about a school subject

PRACTICE 1: THEIR EYES WERE ON THE SKIES

Read the selection, and then answer the questions that follow.

(1)   As young boys, Wilbur (1867–1912) and Orville (1871–1948) Wright sold homemade mechanical toys. In their twenties, the boys made bikes. And in their thirties, they built their own flying machines.

(2)   The Wrights' flying began with gliders. They tested wind-gliders near Kitty Hawk, North Carolina, where breezes were most favorable. But the gliders didn't have quite enough lifting power, so the boys went back to the drawing board. They built a 6-foot (1.8 m) wind tunnel where they tested new wing designs. After building and flying almost 1,000 gliders, they found the right design, then moved on to create a motor-driven aircraft.

(3)   In 1903, Wilbur and Orville spent less than $1,000 to build *Flyer 1*, a gasoline-powered plane. Its wings were 40 feet (12 m) across, and with a pilot aboard, weighed about 750 pounds (340 kg). On December 17, Orville flew *Flyer 1* 120 feet (37 m) for 12 seconds. Later that day, Wilbur flew it 852 feet (260 m) and was airborne for 59 seconds. The age of flight had arrived.

1. You can tell this is nonfiction because
  a. it has imaginary characters.
  b. it has facts about real people and events.
  c. it has dialogue for actors to speak.
  d. it has rhythm and some words rhyme.

2. You would most likely find this kind of writing in a
  a. fairytale.
  b. newspaper.
  c. history textbook.
  d. science fiction story.

3. *My brother Orville and I grew up in Dayton, Ohio. We were always interested in mechanical things, long before we built the first motor-driven plane.* If an author wrote this, you would most likely find it
  a. in a biography.
  b. in an autobiography.
  c. in a play.
  d. in an encyclopedia.

PRACTICE 2: A HELPING HAND—OR TEETH!

Based on a story by Aesop

Read the selection, and then answer the questions that follow.

SCENE 1 [*forest area; enter Mouse*]

MOUSE: I'm famished! I'll just look for some tasty seeds to eat. [*exit*]

LION: [*enter*] Umm! That was a gr-r-reat breakfast! [*yawn*] But now I'm exhausted. I think I'll take a nap. [*lies down and snores softly*]

SCENE 2 [*enter Mouse; doesn't see Lion and bumps into him*]

LION: Wh-Wh-What? [*grabs Mouse*] Well, what have we here?

MOUSE: Oh, great Lion, please don't hurt me. Please, let me go.

LION: Why should I, Mouse? You'd make a yummy little snack!

MOUSE: But someday you may need my help!

LION: Ha-ha, ha-ha! What a laugh! You help *me*? What could a silly, scared little mouse do to help a strong, brave lion like me?

MOUSE: I don't know, but this gianormous forest is full of danger. And small animals can help bigger ones. I'm sure of it!

LION: [*laughs*] You're lucky, Mouse. I'm feeling generous today, so I'll let you go. Besides, I really shouldn't eat between meals!

MOUSE: Oh, thank you, great Lion. You won't be sorry! [*exit*]

LION: What a silly little mouse. Imagine a lion needing the help of a mouse! Ha-ha-ha! [*exit*]

SCENE 3 [*Enter Lion, roaring and tangled in a net*]

LION: ROAR! Oh, no! I'm caught in this hunter's net! What'll I do? ROAR!

MOUSE: [*enter*] What's that noise? Oh, there's someone caught in that net. Wait! I recognize that voice! [*crosses to Lion*] You're the lion that let me go! It looks like you could use some help. Don't worry, I'll get you out.

LION: But what can you do to help?

MOUSE: I'll chew through the ropes with my sharp teeth. [*chews rope*]

LION: Chew away, little Mouse, chew away! I was wrong; a little animal *can* help a big animal. I'm sorry I laughed at you.

MOUSE: There! That hole's big enough, now crawl out of the net, Lion.

LION: I'm free! Thank you, little Mouse, thank you. You saved my life!

MOUSE: That's okay, Lion. I'm glad I could help. After all, you saved *my* life once, remember? But listen . . . I hear the hunters coming.

LION: Let's get out of here . . . my friend! [*Exit Lion and Mouse*]

4. You know this selection is fiction because it
   a. has facts about a forest.
   b. has imaginary talking animals.
   c. has a net and there are real net traps.
   d. is very short.

5. You can identify this selection as a play because it
   a. has stanzas.
   b. is a personal story about real events.
   c. includes facts and statistics about mice.
   d. gives dialogue and directions for actors.

6. Which is the most likely moral, or lesson, of this fable?
   a. Don't count your chickens before they're hatched.
   b. A bird in the hand is worth two in the bush.
   c. Kindness given will be kindness repaid.
   d. Don't put off until tomorrow what you can do today.

7. This play is divided into sections or
   a. scenes.
   b. acts.
   c. stanzas.
   d. locations.

8. The information in square brackets [ ] are
   a. to be spoken by the actors.
   b. facts to tell the audience.
   c. directions for the actors to follow.
   d. all of the above

PRACTICE 3: HEALTH FEATURE: FLU FACTS

Read the selection, and then answer the questions that follow.

(1)   It's that time of year again. Just yesterday two of my friends said, "I was absent last week because I had the flu." Now it's true that lots of people say they have "the flu," but just what is it, anyway?

(2) Influenza, or "the flu," is a serious, contagious respiratory, or breathing, illness. It's caused by a virus and spreads through tiny droplets in the air after someone who has the flu coughs or sneezes. So how do you know if someone has the flu or just a very bad cold? Well, generally, someone who comes down with the flu suddenly:

- has a fever.
- has headaches.
- has muscle and joint pain.
- has a sore throat and a bad cough.
- has a runny or stuffy nose.
- is very fatigued, with barely enough energy to move.

(3) Flu symptoms usually appear one to three days after you've been infected, and you remain contagious to other people for three to four days after your symptoms start. That's why the flu travels through a whole community, like a school.

(4) Most people get better within a week, but the flu can cause some pretty serious complications, like pneumonia. That's especially true for the little kids, the elderly, and anyone who already has breathing problems like asthma.

(5) Antibiotics that kill bacteria can't kill a virus, so doctors don't prescribe them to treat the flu. But there are new anti-flu medicines that can help reduce the seriousness and length of the illness. They have to be taken early, when the symptoms first start. Other than that, the only things you can do to treat the fever, headaches, and muscle pains of the flu is to drink plenty of liquids, take pain relievers, and rest.

(6) Isn't there any way people can protect themselves from getting the flu? Well, it helps to remind others to cover their mouths when they cough or sneeze, and to wash your hands often! But the most effective protection is to get a vaccination, or "flu shot."

(7) Since there are different flu viruses, scientists have to create a vaccine to work on the virus currently circulating. A yearly flu shot is recommended. It provides 70–90% protection against infection for about a year. But even if you do get the flu anyway, your chances of getting serious complications are greatly reduced.

(8)   A flu outbreak in 1918–1919 was worldwide. One-fifth of the world's population was infected and 20–40 million people died. Today people worry about the "Bird Flu." The virus is found mostly in birds, but since 1997 some humans have been infected. So far, only a few hundred people have died from "Bird Flu," but experts say it's only a matter of time before this, or some other flu, causes another pandemic. So take care of yourself . . . and cover that cough!

9. Which is the best clue that this selection is nonfiction?
- **a.** It gives real facts and statistics.
- **b.** It uses the word *you*.
- **c.** It has the words to a song.
- **d.** Some of the words rhyme.

10. Where would you most likely find this selection?
- **a.** in an encyclopedia
- **b.** in a math textbook
- **c.** in a book of fairytales
- **d.** in a magazine

11. This nonfiction selection reads somewhat like fiction because the author
- **a.** tells about a science subject.
- **b.** talks directly to the reader, using the word *you*.
- **c.** explains what flu symptoms are.
- **d.** gives dates and statistics, like percentages.

12. Where would you most likely find the following?
Influenza, a contagious, viral, respiratory illness. Symptoms: fever, headache, muscle/joint pain, sore throat, cough, runny/stuffy nose, fatigue
- **a.** in a cookbook
- **b.** in a mystery story
- **c.** in an encyclopedia
- **d.** in a poem

ANSWERS

1. b
2. c
3. b
4. b
5. d
6. c
7. a
8. c
9. a
10. d
11. b
12. c

author's purpose

My method is to take the utmost trouble to find the right thing to say, and then to say it with the utmost levity.
GEORGE BERNARD SHAW (1856–1950)
IRISH PLAYWRIGHT

In this lesson, you'll discover how to evaluate an author's reason for writing something.

AN AUTHOR'S PURPOSE is why he or she wrote something. It might be to:

- inform readers.

   Example
   Every president except George Washington has lived in the White House. However, Washington did help design the building.

- teach readers how to do something.

   Example
   To do a waltz jump, take off from the outside edge of one skate, make a half turn, and land on the outside edge of the other blade.

- entertain or amuse readers.

   Example
   The cat leaped just as Pam came in with a bowl of milk. Pam went down and the milk went up . . . and then down, on her head!

• persuade readers to do something.

> **Example**
>
> Good citizens donate old clothes to charity. It may be hard to give up a favorite outgrown sweater, but we have needy people in our community. Why not let *your* old sweater keep another kid warm this winter instead of hanging it in the back of your closet?

Sometimes an author has more than one purpose, such as wanting to inform readers but be entertaining at the same time!

To identify an author's purpose, ask yourself questions like:

Did I find out something new?

Did I learn how to do something?

How did this make me feel happy, sad, scared, or excited?

Did the author try to get me to do something or think a certain way?

PRACTICE 1: RIPPLES OF ENERGY

Read the selection, and then answer the questions that follow.

(1)   A wave is any movement that carries energy. Some waves carry energy through water. Others carry energy through gases, like air, or solid materials. If you drop a rock into a pool of water, a wave, or ripple of energy, skims across the pool's surface. In the same way, an underwater earthquake can release energy into ocean water. Then it carries a giant wave, or tsunami, across the surface until it hits land.

(2)   If you hear a clap of thunder, sound waves (or vibrations) have carried the crashing BOOM to your ears. Sound waves speed through the air at about 1,100 feet (335 meters) per second.

(3)   Light also travels through the air in waves. They travel at more than 186,000 miles (300 million meters) per second. So the light waves from a flash of lightning reach your eyes before that clap of thunder reaches your ears!

(4)   Electrons travel in waves, too. They move back and forth in a solid wire, sending waves of electricity so you can turn on a light during the storm!

1. What is the author's most important purpose for writing the selection?
   a. to persuade readers to throw rocks into the water
   b. to entertain readers with the legend of Wally Wave
   c. to teach readers how to use a surfboard to ride waves
   d. to inform readers about different kinds of waves

2. Which question could best help someone figure out this author's purpose?
   a. Did the author give me information?
   b. Did I learn how to make an electric light?
   c. Did the selection make me feel sad or scared?
   d. Did the author want me to make waves?

3. Which might also have been an author's purpose for this selection?
   a. to teach readers why people wave at one another
   b. to inform readers about gravity and magnetic pull
   c. to persuade readers to study more about tsunamis
   d. to entertain readers with a little humor

PRACTICE 2: PEOPLE WHO NEED PEOPLE

Read the selection, and then answer the questions that follow.

(1)   Everyone needs help sometime. Humans depend on one another. That's why communities everywhere have special people to lend a helping hand to anyone who needs it.

(2)   For example, what would our citizens do without a community fire department? If a home catches on fire, as the Jackson place did last week, it might be destroyed and the inhabitants hurt . . . or worse. We're so fortunate to have trained firefighters to come to the rescue and put out the fire, safely. If the fire department hadn't come so quickly, the Jacksons might have lost everything.

(3)   And what about our local police who protect our families, our homes, and our belongings? The police have helped so many families this past year, especially rescuing people and pets and protecting our property after the flood.

(4)   Think about all the other service workers we have in this community. We have sanitation workers who collect trash and keep our community clean. We have road workers who put up and repair traffic signs and fix potholes in the streets to protect not just us, but the tires on our cars! And where would this community be without the teachers in our school and the doctors, nurses, and technicians in our community clinics?

(5)   We benefit so much from all these tireless workers who keep our community running. But these services are expensive. As citizens, we pay taxes, it's true, and some of the taxes go toward buying the services we need. But today, there's just not enough money. Times are hard and the economy has slowed. Plants are closing and people are losing their jobs and homes. But citizens still need services!

(6)   Many service workers are thinking of leaving and going to other communities where they'll be paid a better wage, one that allows them to support their families. They can't afford to live here anymore . . . and we can't afford to let them leave.

(7)   We need these people in the community. So join with us today as we petition for changes to our tax system that will allow our community to keep more of the tax dollars to invest in service workers who live right here in the community. Please sign our petition now, and be sure to vote for Proposition 6X1 on Election Day!

4. What is the author's most important purpose for writing the selection?
   a. to entertain readers with an exciting story about a flood
   b. to persuade readers to sign a petition about taxes
   c. to teach readers how to use the new voting machines
   d. to inform readers about what firefighters do

5. Which question could best help someone figure out this author's purpose?
   a. Did the author make me laugh?
   b. Did the author teach me what to do in case of fire?
   c. Did the author inform me about how to become a teacher?
   d. Did the author want me to do something?

6. If the last paragraph had NOT been written, what do you think the author's purpose would have been?
   a. to explain to citizens who the Jacksons are
   b. to thank citizens for paying taxes
   c. to remind citizens about the many services they have available
   d. to inform readers about the dangers of potholes

7. Why do you think the author believes readers will sign the petition?
   a. because they like firefighters
   b. because they are members of the community
   c. because they have cars
   d. because they need stop signs

8. How does the first sentence give a clue about the author's purpose?
   a. It signals that the author may ask readers to do something to help others.
   b. It signals that the author is talking about math.
   c. It signals that the author is not American.
   d. It signals that the selection is fiction.

PRACTICE 3: TIME AFTER TIME

Read the selection, and then answer the questions that follow.

(1) "I'm so tired," Sabrina said.

(2) "But it's only Monday!" Jake exclaimed. "You can't be tired after that long holiday weekend we had!"

(3) "It all depends," grumbled Sabrina. "You and your dad went skiing, didn't you? I'll bet you had a blast!"

(4) "We spent hours on the slopes," Jake said with a smile. "What did you do?"

(5) "Do? Do? I had so much to do that I didn't have any time for fun!" Sabrina griped, kicking a stone to emphasize her unhappiness.

(6) "Sorry I asked!" Jake countered. "What took up all your time?"

(7) "First of all, my homework," said Sabrina with disgust.

(8) "Homework? We didn't have any homework!" Jake announced.

(9) Sabrina lowered her eyes. "Well, maybe I put off some old homework . . . our science projects are due tomorrow, and I never got around to doing mine."

(10) "You're kidding!" Jake said. "You hadn't even started it?"

(11) "No," sighed Sabrina. "So I had to go to the library and on the Internet to do research, then outline the report and write it!"

(12) "Hi!" called Mike and Sarah. Sarah told about her trip to visit her aunt in Boston and Mike announced that his hockey team won and was going to the championships. "Hey, I didn't see you at the game, Sabrina," he added. "Did you go away for the weekend, too?"

(13) Sabrina gave a dramatic sigh, "No," she groaned, "I was too busy."

(14) "Doing what?" asked Sarah.

(15) "You'll be sorry you asked," whispered Jake as Sabrina began.

(16) Sabrina moaned about her forgotten science project, helping her dad clean the yard, and helping to do the laundry. "Oh, I do that, too," replied Sarah. "I read while I wait for the stuff to come out of the machines."

(17) "But you can't *go* anywhere or *do* anything until its done!" Sabrina sighed. "Then I had to baby-sit my little cousin, Max the Horror, for an hour!"

(18) "So you spent time doing all that stuff," announced Jake, "but you had a whole three days! Maybe you're thinking too much time about the time you *didn't* have instead of looking for fun things you did do!"

(19) "Well, I did watch TV and go to the mall," Sabrina mused. "And I went to see that new movie. I guess you're right, Jake. I was just frustrated and mad at myself because I hadn't done my science report earlier."

(20) At school, Sabrina said, "Mr. Hart will probably assign the next science project to be handed in after spring vacation. If he does, I won't waste a millisecond getting started! Then I can really enjoy my next time off!"

(21) Jake smiled, "We'll see, Miss Put-it-off-till-tomorrow! We'll see!"

9. What is the author's purpose for writing the selection?
   a. to inform readers about science reports
   b. to persuade readers to do a science project
   c. to entertain readers with a fiction story
   d. to teach readers how to schedule their time

10. Which question could best help someone figure out this author's purpose?
   a. Did the author give me new information about a school topic?
   b. Did the author teach me how to make something?
   c. Did the author ask me to do anything?
   d. Did the author tell me a story about kids my age?

11. If the following had been added at the end of the selection, what do you think the author's purpose would have been for adding it?

So remember, dear reader, don't procrastinate. Never postpone until tomorrow what you can do today!

   a. to teach readers that *procrastinate* means "postpone"

   b. to persuade readers to budget their time

   c. to amuse readers with a silly saying

   d. to inform readers that tomorrow will be better

ANSWERS

1. d
2. a
3. c
4. b
5. d
6. c
7. b
8. a
9. c
10. d
11. b

tone and style

"When I use a word," Humpty Dumpty said
in rather a scornful tone, "it means just what I choose
it to mean—neither more nor less."
LEWIS CARROLL (1832–1898)
ENGLISH AUTHOR, *ALICE'S ADVENTURES IN WONDERLAND*

In this lesson, you'll discover that how an author puts all the words together in a selection can change the meaning and feelings you get from it.

AN AUTHOR SETS a purpose for writing, and then chooses words to express ideas. The words set a **tone** that, just like someone's tone of voice, will convey a feeling of suspense, excitement, happiness, sadness, anger, mystery, humor, or annoyance. Choosing the right words can make a selection funny, sad, creepy, serious, mysterious, scary, or fanciful. Different parts of a selection may convey different feelings. But there should be one clear tone for the whole selection.

An author's **style** is his or her distinctive way of connecting ideas. You can easily spot some authors' styles. Like Dr. Seuss . . . everyone recognizes his rhyming and made-up words! It may not be so easy to recognize other authors' styles until you read a few of their selections. Then you begin to spot the length and difficulty of the sentences they use and their choices of descriptive words. Their writing may be informal or formal, friendly or bitter, fanciful or scientific, comical or dramatic, playful or serious.

The author's tone and style create an overall mood, the feeling you get when you read the selection. For example, see how the author's tone and style create a mysterious, frightening feeling in this scenario.

The sliver of moon disappeared behind the clouds, leaving us in the dark as we crept closer to the old house. The gusting wind whipped the shutters, slamming them against the wood siding. Suddenly I saw a flickering light in the upstairs window. Behind it was the face of a creature so hideous that I cannot describe it!

PRACTICE 1: SAVING ELECTRICITY

Read the selection, and then answer the questions that follow.

(1)   Many power plants use fossil fuels, like coal and oil, to produce electricity. They formed more than millions of years ago from the remains of ancient plants and animals and can't be replaced . . . unless we want to wait million of years more! So it's crucial to use electricity wisely. You can help. Look for these and other places where electricity's being wasted . . . then stop wasting it!

- Close the refrigerator door quickly.
- Let your hair dry naturally!
- Run a dishwasher or washing machine only when full.
- Turn off lights when not in use.
- Unplug TVs, DVD players, and other appliances that have clocks when not in use—they continue to draw energy to display time, even when switched off!
- Unplug phone chargers when not in use—they draw small amounts of energy all the time if you don't!

1. What is the tone of the selection?
   a. comical
   b. serious
   c. disrespectful
   d. mysterious

2. Why do you think the author chose to use the word *crucial* instead of its synonym *important*?
   a. to add a light touch to the text
   b. to show disagreement about energy consumption
   c. to imply that there should be no power plants
   d. to stress the urgent need to conserve resources

3. Part of the author's style includes the use of

    a. words in parenthesis ( ).

    b. very short sentences.

    c. ellipses(. . .).

    d. foreign words.

PRACTICE 1: ADAPTED FROM *THE LAST LEAF*

by O'Henry

Read the selection, and then answer the questions that follow.

(1) Julia and Marissa moved into a small New York apartment, hoping to start careers as fashion designers. Other people in the building were also artists, and quite friendly. When winter came, many of them suffered with colds and flu, and several, including Julia, were caught in the grip of pneumonia.

(2) The illness made it hard for Julia to breathe. She slept a lot and when she was awake, she sat quietly in a chair, staring out the window and sighing. The constant struggle sapped her will to live and she refused the food Marissa fixed for her. Finally, Marissa asked the doctor if Julia would ever get better. He hesitated, then said, "Her only chance is to *want* to get better. The human body's a wonderful thing . . . it can heal, but we must help it by believing that it will. I'm afraid that without a change of heart, she won't make it."

(3) Marissa hid her tears as she tried to interest Julia in sketches of spring fashions. But Julia just muttered. "Eleven, ten, nine," then, "eight, seven, six."

(4) "What are you counting?" asked Marissa looking in the direction her friend was staring. All she could see was an old oak tree with almost no leaves.

(5) "The leaves," murmured Julia. "When they're gone, I will go, too."

(6) "What are you talking about?" Marissa exclaimed. "Leaves have nothing to do with your getting better! You have to *want* to get better! I'm shutting these curtains, and we're not talking about this again!"

(7) After Julia fell asleep, Marissa went to Johann, an old painter who lived in the building. Tearfully, she told him her plan and he agreed. All night, Marissa heard the wind howling mournfully and rain splashing against the windowpane. She knew the remaining leaves would be blown away by morning.

(8) When Julia awoke, Marissa opened the curtains to reveal one leaf remaining on the tree. "It's the last leaf," she sighed. "I was sure they'd all be gone."

(9) All day the leaf clung to the tree, despite the beating wind. Julia watched intently as the leaf refused to leave the safety of the branch and fall, dead to the ground. Finally, she took a deep breath . . . then another . . . and called to Marissa, "Could I please have some toast? I need to get my strength back. I can't just waste my life away. . . . We're going to be great designers someday!"

(10) Later, when Julia had greatly improved, Marissa whispered, "I need to tell you that . . . Johann has pneumonia. The super found him in the rain a few days ago. He'd just painted an oak leaf on that tree . . . because the last leaf had fallen."

(11) "Oh, Marissa," cried Julia. "He saved my life by making me want to be strong like the leaf and live. Now we must do something for him." And so they did.

4. What is the overall tone of the selection?
   a. angry
   b. comical
   c. mysterious
   d. emotional

5. What is the tone of the last paragraph?
   a. frightening
   b. hopeful
   c. irritated
   d. comical

6. Why do you think the author chose to use the words *caught in the grip of*?
   a. to imply that pneumonia squeezed the life, or breath, from its victims
   b. to show that pneumonia and flu were alike
   c. to imply that pneumonia was not serious
   d. to state that pneumonia is contagious

7. Read these words from the selection: *the remaining leaves would be blown away by morning.* Which might the author most likely have considered using instead of *morning*?
   a. the next day
   b. for sure
   c. daybreak
   d. after all

8. What is the author's overall style?

a. friendly

b. mocking

c. playful

d. creepy

PRACTICE 2: EXCERPTED AND ADAPTED FROM *ALICE'S ADVENTURES IN WONDERLAND*

by Lewis Carroll

Read the selection, and then answer the questions that follow.

(1) The Cheshire Cat gave Alice directions to the March Hare's home. She had not gone very far before she noticed the house. Well, she thought it must be the right house. The chimneys were shaped like long rabbit ears. The roof was thatched with rabbit fur. It was so large a house that she was scared to keep walking closer.

(2) She worked up enough courage and walked closer. A table was set out under a tree in front of the house, and the March Hare and Mad Hatter were having tea. A Dormouse was sitting between them, fast asleep. The table was large, but the three were all crowded together at one corner of it.

(3) "No room! No room!" they cried out when they saw Alice coming.

(4) "There's *plenty* of room!" said Alice firmly, as she sat down in a large armchair at one end of the table.

(5) "It wasn't very civil of you to sit down without being invited," said the March Hare.

(6) "I didn't know it was *your* table," said Alice. "It's laid for a great many more than three."

7) "Your hair wants cutting," said the Hatter. He had been looking at Alice for some time with great curiosity, and this was his first speech.

(8) "You should learn not to make personal remarks," Alice said with some severity. "It's very rude."

(9) The Hatter opened his eyes very wide on hearing this, but all he *said* was, "Why is a raven like a writing desk?"

(10) "Come, we shall have some fun now!" thought Alice. "I'm glad they've begun asking riddles." She added aloud, "I believe I can guess that."

(11) "Do you mean you think you can find the answer to it?" said the March Hare.

(12) "Exactly so," said Alice.

(13) "Then you should say what you mean," the March Hare went on.

(14) "I do," Alice hastily replied. "At least—at least I mean what I say—that's the same thing, you know."

(15) "Not the same thing a bit!" said the Hatter. "You might just as well say that 'I see what I eat' is the same thing as 'I eat what I see'!"

(16) "You might just as well say," added the March Hare, "that 'I like what I get' is the same thing as 'I get what I like'!"

(17) "You might just as well say," added the Dormouse, who seemed to be talking in his sleep, "that 'I breathe when I sleep' is the same thing as 'I sleep when I breathe'!"

(18) "It *is* the same thing with you," said the Hatter, and here the conversation dropped, and the party sat silent for a minute.

9. What is the tone of the selection?
  a. scary
  b. fanciful
  c. technical
  d. electrifying

10. The author probably wants readers to
  a. become angry at the Dormouse.
  b. be frightened of the Mad Hatter.
  c. forgive the Cheshire Cat.
  d. feel sorry for poor, confused Alice.

11. The author's style includes the use of
  a. many technical terms.
  b. only extremely long sentences.
  c. words in all capital letters for emphasis.
  d. a rhyming pattern.

12. Read these words from the selection: *It wasn't very civil of you.* Which might the author most likely have considered using instead of *civil*?

   a. polite

   b. urbane

   c. boorish

   d. sweet

ANSWERS

  1. b

  2. d

  3. c

  4. d

  5. b

  6. a

  7. c

  8. a

  9. b

10. d

11. c

12. d

text features

One writer, for instance, excels at a plan or a title-page, another
works away the body of the book, and a third is a dab at an index.

OLIVER GOLDSMITH (1728–1774)
IRISH POET AND PLAYWRIGHT

In this lesson, you'll discover some ways that authors try to help you find and
better understand the information they present.

TEXT FEATURES ARE special ways authors present information to help their
readers better understand the material. You might say these features are like
maps—they help you find your way through a maze of information! Fiction
selections have features, but more about them later. Right now, we'll concentrate
on the text features you find in nonfiction.

SOME COMMON NONFICTION TEXT FEATURES

boldface words	**dark type** used to emphasize important vocabulary
bulleted list	listing of important facts set off from regular text
caption	text with a graphic that gives details about it
contents	lists each book chapter in sequence and the page on which it starts
glossary	mini-dictionary at the end of a book that defines each boldface word
heading	name of a selection, chapter, or section
index	alphabetical list at the back of a book identifying important ideas in the book and pages on which each idea is mentioned
italicized words	*slanted italic* type used for book titles, foreign words, a word as an example of a word (the word *word*), or for emphasis
sidebar	information placed beside the main text, often in a box, that expands on an idea in the text
subhead	divides a selection into parts and tells what each part is about
title	name of a whole book

Skim and scan books and articles for any features before you begin to read. They can help you predict what the selection is about and what you can expect to get out of reading it. Planning ahead like this as an active reader can help you not only increase your understanding of what you read, but retain the information longer.

PRACTICE 1: DREAMS

Read the selection, and then answer the questions that follow.

(1)   A dream is a story a sleeper watches or takes part in. It's filled with images, sounds, odors, and emotions. On waking, a sleeper may remember only what happened right before waking up. No one can recall every dream, but everyone dreams, even though some people may tell you they don't. They really do dream; they just don't remember any of their dreams!

Looking for Meaning

(2)   Events in dreams are imaginary, but they're related to real experiences in the sleeper's life. Sometimes dreams are realistic. If you spent the day at the beach, you might dream of the ocean that night.

(3)   Other times, dreams can be **symbolic**. For example, a teenage girl has a dream about walking a dog. As they walk, the dog pulls faster and faster until the girl tumbles down a hill. The dream might symbolize that the dreamer is so busy with school, sports, parties, and family that she feels she has no control over her life. It's as if life (the dog) is pulling the teen too fast in too many directions!

1. Which text feature does the author use to divide the article into parts?
   a. glossary
   b. index
   c. subhead
   d. italics

2. Where would a reader look for a definition of the boldface word *symbolic*?
   a. the title
   b. the index
   c. the contents
   d. the glossary

3. Why is DREAMS at the top of the selection set in capital letters?
   a. because it's the caption
   b. because it's the heading
   c. because it's in italics
   d. because it's part of a bulleted list

PRACTICE 2: MOVING ON

Read the selection, and then answer the questions that follow.

(1)   Winter in some places is very cold. Snow covers the ground and ponds and lakes freeze. Many animals can't find the food they need to survive, so they migrate—from the Latin *migrans* "to move from one place to another." They go to warmer places where food is still accessible and stay there until spring, then migrate back home. Diverse animals migrate in diverse ways. Here are just a few.

By Air

(2)   To find warmer places, some birds fly more than 3,000 miles. In spring, they fly home, build nests, and lay eggs. The following autumn, the baby birds will migrate, too.

(3)   Some butterflies fly south over 1,000 miles for the winter. As they fly back home in spring, they stop along the way to lay eggs. The new butterflies that hatch continue the trip north.

(4)   To get where flowers are still blooming, some bats migrate more than 1,000 miles across the desert. The bats feed on the **nectar** from the flowers.

By Water

(5)   Pods of whales live off the coast of Massachusetts, a place that has cold and snowy winters. So the whales swim 3,500 miles south, to warmer water off the island of Bermuda. There they have their young, and in spring, they all swim back home.

(6)   Elephant seals migrate about 21,000 miles roundtrip every year. They travel back and forth between California and Alaska, following the weather . . . and the food.

By Land

(7)   Herds of bighorn sheep in Canada and the United States migrate shorter distances up and down mountains. In summer, there's plenty of grass on mountaintops, but in winter, the ground's covered with snow. So the sheep climb down the mountain where there are still shrubs and other small plants to eat, and in spring, migrate back up to the peaks.

(8)   Caribou that live in the Arctic migrate when the snow gets really deep. They move hundreds of miles to a place where there's less snow. Then they can sniff out, uncover, and eat the tender plants that still grow under the snow.

(9)   What animals migrate from or to the area where you live? Look for movement in spring and fall. Record what you observe.

4. What is the purpose of the subhead "By Land"?
   a. to tell what the next part of the selection will be about
   b. to tell why whales migrate
   c. to put words in alphabetical order
   d. to introduce a sidebar

5. A reader can use the glossary to find out
   a. the page on which this passage starts.
   b. the meaning of the boldface word *nectar*.
   c. the title of the book.
   d. the name of the next selection.

6. The word *migrans* is in italics because it
   a. looks pretty that way.
   b. is the name of a book.
   c. explains what a pod is.
   d. is a foreign word.

7. In an index, the word *caribou* would be
   a. somewhere between *bats* and *birds*.
   b. somewhere between *butterflies* and *elephant seals*.
   c. somewhere between *sheep* and *whales*.
   d. somewhere between *Bighorn sheep* and *butterflies*.

8. Which text feature did the author NOT use?
   a. heading
   b. subhead
   c. sidebar
   d. boldface type

9. What information does the heading tell about the selection?
   a. that it's about someone living in a large city
   b. that it's about crops grown on American farms
   c. that it's about animals in a zoo
   d. that it's about someone or something moving somewhere

PRACTICE 3: PARTIAL TO PEANUTS

Read the selection, and then answer the questions that follow.

(1) When is a nut NOT a nut? When it's a PEAnut! That's right; the peaNUT is a **legume**, like a pea or bean, with its seeds inside a pod. Peanuts grow in many different places around the world and are called different names including:

   - ground nuts
   - pindars
   - goobers
   - earth nuts

(2) It makes sense to call them "ground nuts" or "earth nuts," because they grow underground in well-drained, sandy soil!

Road to America

(3) More than 3,500 years ago, South American Indians in Brazil and Peru first grew peanuts. Hundreds of years later, Spanish explorers ate some, then took some back home to plant. Later, people took peanuts from Spain to Africa, where they quickly became a **staple**.

(4) In the 1700s, some Africans brought peanuts to America. They ate some and planted some. Along with sandy soil, peanuts need plenty of sunshine, water, and four or five months of warm weather—just what's available in our southern states. So by 1800, groundnuts were growing all over the South. And today, with about 40,000 peanut farms, the United States is the world's third-largest peanut producer.

The Peanut Man

(5) George Washington Carver is often called "the peanut wizard" because he not only helped to make peanuts "big business," he found many different ways to use them. Born around 1864, Carver worked a lot with plants as he was growing up. When he grew up, he taught about farming and plants in Alabama.

(6) In 1914, southern cotton crops were destroyed by insects. The farmers had no income, so Carver convinced them to plant peanuts. And he looked for ways to use every part of the peanut plant. Before long, he'd made 325 different things from ground nuts, including coffee, cheese, ink, glue, face powder, soap, shampoo, mayonnaise, medicine, hand lotion, rubber, and ice cream!

IT'S A FACT: Circus owner P.T. Barnum first sold peanuts to his show-goers more than 100 years ago. Soon the snack showed up at ballparks, where today vendors may sell as many as 7,000 bags in one day!

10. The author gives information about ballpark peanuts in
    a. the heading.
    b. a sidebar.
    c. the table of contents.
    d. a caption.

11. The first subhead tells readers that the next part is about
    a. what you can make from peanuts.
    b. George Washington Carver.
    c. why the peanut is not a nut.
    d. how peanuts got to America.

12. A reader can use the glossary to find out
    a. the meanings of *legume* and *staple*.
    b. the meanings of *pod* and *goobers*.
    c. the meanings of *pintars* and *pod*.
    d. the meanings of *mayonnaise* and *pod*.

13. The title "Partial to Peanuts" is
    a. an index.
    b. a heading.
    c. a caption.
    d. a subhead.

14. How does the author use a bulleted list?
- **a.** to tell which counties grow peanuts
- **b.** to tell the names of famous peanut farmers
- **c.** to list the amounts of peanuts grown each year
- **d.** to tell some names people call peanuts

ANSWERS

1. c
2. d
3. b
4. a
5. b
6. d
7. b
8. c
9. d
10. b
11. d
12. a
13. b
14. d

graphics

One picture is worth ten thousand words.
FRED R. BARNARD (1920s)
AMERICAN ADVERTISING MANAGER

In this lesson, you'll take a look at the way authors use special features to give you information visually!

IN THE LAST lesson, you saw how authors use text features to help you understand what you read. Well, authors also use **graphic** features to help clarify ideas or give readers additional information to that given in the text. Here are some common graphic features you may find in fiction and nonfiction:

COMMON GRAPHIC FEATURES

chart	list of information
diagram	drawing that shows arrangement and labeled parts of a whole
flowchart	series of boxes and arrows to show step-by-step progression
graph	shows the relationship between numbers of things
illustration	drawing of people, a place, an object, or an event
map	drawing of part of Earth to show features like oceans, countries, mountains, or roads
photo	printed image of people, a place, an object, or an event
realia	detailed photo of a real historical object, like a poster, map, or newspaper article
table	a systematic arrangement of data in rows and columns
timeline	lists facts along a line in the order in which they happened

Before you read a book or article, skim and scan to look for graphics. Use them to try to predict what the material is all about.

PRACTICE 1: AT THE LIBRARY

Read the selection and graphic, and then answer the questions that follow.

(1) "I can't find anything at this library!" said Mia's brother.

(2) Mia took a book off the shelf. "It's easy," she said. "Look. The part of the book you see on the shelf is the spine, and this number at the bottom is the book's address—where it 'lives' in the library. This is fiction. Fiction's arranged in ABC order by author's last name. See, *F* for Fiction and *Ca* for the first two letters of the name, *Carroll*."

(3) "But what about nonfiction?" her brother asked.

(4) "It's arranged by subject," Mia said. "Libraries use the Dewey decimal system . . . there's a period to divide numbers into parts," she added, in case he didn't know. "Nonfiction's divided into 10 large groups, from 000 to 900. Then each group's divided into many smaller ones."

(5) Mia's brother still looked confused so she showed him a poster on one of the bookcases. "Look, the library lists the groups for you."

(6) Just then, Mr. Reyes, the librarian came by. He smiled, "And if you still don't find what you want, ask a librarian . . . that's what we're here for!"

DEWEY DECIMAL SYSTEM

(10 groups and sample subjects)

000 General Knowledge
   Encyclopedias, Newspapers, Almanacs

100 Psychology and Philosophy
   Feelings, Logic, Making Friends, Optical Illusions

200 Religions and Mythology
   Bible stories, Native American myths

300 Social Sciences and Folklore
   Families, Careers, Manners, Money, Customs, Festivals

400 Languages and Grammar
   English, Spanish, Sign Language, Chinese

500 Math and Science
   Subtraction, Division, Animals, Oceans, Fossils, Planets

| 600 Medicine and Technology |
| Health, Computers, The Human Body, Telephones |

| 700 Arts and Recreation |
| Crafts, Games, Jokes, Music, Sports |

| 800 Literature |
| Shakespeare, Plays, Poems, Writing |

| 900 Geography and History |
| Native Americans, World Nations, Biographies |

1. The chart shows a list of
   a. the ten groups of fiction books available at the library.
   b. the ten reasons to get your own library card.
   c. the ten alphabetical listings for fiction.
   d. the ten groups in the Dewey Decimal System and some sample topics.

2. According to the graphic, in which section would you find a book about swimming?
   a. 400
   b. 600
   c. 700
   d. 900

3. From the graphic, you know the 300 section would most likely have a book about
   a. Olympic figure skaters.
   b. the respiratory system.
   c. holidays around the world.
   d. former U.S. presidents.

PRACTICE 2: MIGHTY MUSCLES

Read the selection, and then answer the questions that follow. Use the graphics to help you.

(1)   What would we do without muscles? They're what help us move and stay on the go. But just what are they?

(2)   Muscles are made of long strings of fiber. They help you survive. When you eat, you swallow, right? Yes, thanks to some muscular action. Then the food goes down through your stomach and intestines, where more muscles squeeze, mix, and break down the food, then get rid of it.

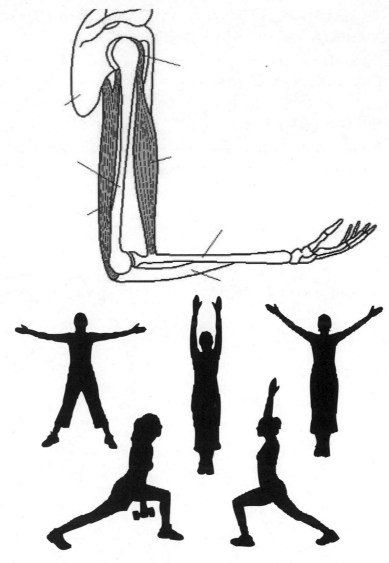

(3)   And how do you get the oxygen it needs to keep you alive? You breathe
       it in, thanks to a muscle. Your diaphragm, a muscle right under your
       lungs, pulls the good air in through your nose and mouth and sends it
       down to your lungs. They move it to your heart, a big muscle that trans-
       mits oxygen-rich blood throughout your body. Then, when the oxygen's
       been used up and carbon dioxide produced, your diaphragm pushes the
       bad gas away as you breathe out!

(4)   When you push or pull, you use muscles. Some come in pairs. For exam-
       ple, your upper arm has biceps and triceps. These muscles stretch between
       one bone in your upper arm and one in your lower arm. When your biceps
       contract, or get shorter, they pull on the lower bone. That makes your lower
       arm move upward and helps you lift things, like heavy textbooks. When

your triceps contract, your biceps relax to let your arm straighten and can push down.

(5)   The more you push and pull your muscles, the stronger they get. Skating, swimming, dancing, and other kinds of exercises can help you build muscle in your whole body. Such exercises require your body to work many muscles at the same time.

(6)   Think about what your muscles can do. Touch your toes. Bend your elbow. Take a breath. Say "thanks" to your muscles!

4. What kind of graphic does the author use to show the biceps and triceps?
   a. a photo
   b. a graph
   c. a timeline
   d. a diagram

5. To show people exercising, the author uses
   a. a map.
   b. an illustration.
   c. a flowchart.
   d. a photo.

6. How does the graphic of the biceps and triceps clarify the text?
   a. by showing where muscles are attached to arm bones
   b. by showing how high an arm can reach
   c. by comparing the lengths of bones in the arm
   d. by listing all the parts of the digestive system

7. Which other graphic would best clarify information in the article?
   a. a timeline showing the ages from childhood to old age
   b. a flowchart showing how muscles move food through the digestive system
   c. a map showing where local hospitals are located
   d. a photo of someone eating

8. What are the words that identify parts on a diagram called?
   a. memos
   b. titles
   c. labels
   d. quotations

9. Which would be the best chart to support the article?
   a. list of name and function of muscles: *skeletal* move limbs; *cardiac* pump blood; *smooth* do many jobs in other organs
   b. list books about nutrition and where to get them
   c. list bones in the leg and foot
   d. list foods by calorie amounts

PRACTICE 3: CONDOR COMEBACK

Read the selection, and then answer the questions that follow. Use the graphics to help you.

(1)   The California Condor is the largest flying land bird in North America and one of its endangered species. It's an unmistakable bird; you'd recognize it immediately. Its body is about 52 inches (132 cm) long, and it usually weighs 18–23 pounds (8–10 k). Most of its giant body is covered with black feathers, but there are patches of white on the undersides of its wings. A ring of black feathers covers the bottom of its neck, which is featherless and yellow-orange, like its head.

(2)   Condors have a wingspan of about 9 feet (2.7 m) and make their homes high in the mountains, where updrafts of wind provide perfect conditions for soaring. These powerful fliers flap their wings a few times, then glide and soar silently, looking for food on the ground far below. They spend a lot of time resting on high cliffs, but don't build their nests there. Instead, they lay their eggs in caves or among high rocks. A female condor lays just one egg every two years.

(3)   Once thousands of these giant birds flew above the mountains along the Pacific coastline. Then humans entered the picture and the California condor's habitat, and very existence, changed. Overhunting and the building of cities and roads threatened the condors with extinction. By 1890, there were only 600 birds left, and the numbers continued to dwindle.

(4)   Although it was illegal to kill a condor, some people still did. And condors faced the danger of accidentally flying into wires or buildings along their flyways. But their biggest problem came from chemicals. Ranchers used chemicals to stop coyotes that stole sheep. Since condors are part of the

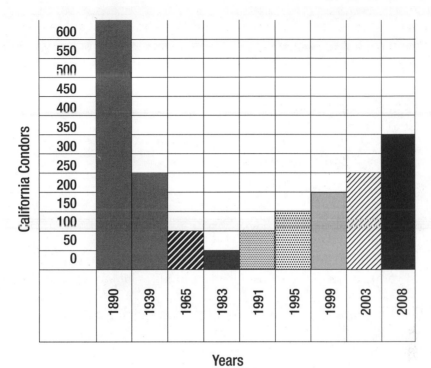

Years

vulture family, they feed on dead animals. So, unfortunately, the chemicals also poisoned the birds when they fed on dead coyotes. By the 1980s, it was obvious that the California Condor wouldn't survive without help from people.

(5)   The chemical that killed condors was banned, and scientists captured the last wild condors to protect and breed them. Their offspring would later be returned to the wild. It took years, but through this captive breeding, California Condors have been reintroduced to the coastal mountains of California and the Grand Canyon area of northern Arizona. The fabulous fliers

Where California Condors soar today

have come back from the edge of extinction and once again soar stylishly through the sky.

10. How does the illustration of a condor help readers?
    a. lists the cities where condors are found
    b. shows what is being described in the text
    c. shows the step-by-step process for capturing a condor
    d. labels each part of the animal

11. What information does the graph compare?
    a. the wingspans of different California Condors
    b. the population of California in different years
    c. the heights of mountains in different parts of California
    d. the population of California Condors in different years

12. Which graphic does the author use to show where the condors live?
    a. a graph
    b. a map
    c. a diagram
    d. a flowchart

13. According to the graph, in which year were there the least California Condors?
    a. 1939
    b. 1965
    c. 1983
    d. 2008

ANSWERS

1. d
2. b
3. c
4. d
5. b
6. a
7. b
8. c
9. a
10. b
11. d
12. b
13. c

SECTION 3

organization of text

PUTTING THE WORDS TOGETHER

Authors write for different reasons and in different ways, but they all want their readers to get the most out of what they've written. So authors organize, or structure, their text in a certain way to get their message to readers as clearly as possible. The author might tell a story step by step, in the order in which the things happened. Another author may tell a tale by comparing the looks and actions of the characters. Still another author may continually ask questions in the text, knowing the answers are there . . . somewhere. There are many methods an author can use, and in this section of the book, you'll learn a few. You'll discover how to

- identify the main idea and supporting details.
- interpret a sequence of events.
- analyze causes and effects to predict outcomes.
- locate details that are compared or contrasted.
- distinguish the difference between a fact and an opinion.
- recognize how questions connect you to the text.
- classify problems and solutions.
- identify inferences.
- draw conclusions.
- identify the most important parts to summarize.

Graphic organizers, like cause-and-effect charts and Venn diagrams that let you compare and contrast ideas, can help you organize your ideas as you read. These visual tools can help you keep track of ideas, see how ideas are related, and remember more of what you read. More about graphic organizers later.

main idea and supporting details

Beware of the man who won't be bothered with details.
WILLIAM FEATHER (1908–1976)
AMERICAN PUBLISHER AND AUTHOR

In this lesson, you'll discover that an author communicates one big idea and gives details about it.

THE MAIN IDEA is what a selection's mostly about—the most important thing the author wants readers to know. Other facts in the selection are details that support, or tell more about, the main idea. Sometimes the main idea is stated directly.

Example
Grass is one of Earth's most useful plants. Most people think of it as the stuff that grows in the yard and needs to be mowed, but there are thousands of different kinds. Wheat, rice, and other grains are grasses that help people and animals exist!

The main idea is stated: Grass is a useful plant. But sometimes you have to find the main idea yourself. To do that, use information from the text to figure it out.

Example
In 1483, Italian artist Leonardo da Vinci sketched a flying machine. He was also a scientist and fascinated by movement. His sketch showed a screw-like wing made of stiff linen. He never got it off the ground, but a real helicopter like it flew almost 500 years later!

The main idea is that Leonardo da Vinci designed the first helicopter more than 500 years ago. That's what the author most wants you to remember.

In the first example, supporting details are that wheat, rice, and other grains are useful grasses, and people and animals need grasses. In the second example, details are the year he drew the design, that it was a flying machine, what it looked like, and when the first real helicopter flew. Each detail supports or expands on the main idea.

In longer selections, each chapter or section may have its own main idea, but there's just one central idea for the whole selection. Sometimes the title can help you figure out the main idea. And you may find that some details add interest but aren't necessary to finding the main idea, like the fact that da Vinci was fascinated by movement, so they are not "supporting" details.

PRACTICE 1: A MUSICAL MOUSE

Read the selection, and then answer the questions that follow.

(1)   There are many different kinds of mice. Some are good swimmers; others like to swing from trees by their tails. And one kind, the white-footed mouse, is not only a good swimmer and tree climber, but it's also quite musical!

(2)   This minute, furry creature's body is about 8 inches (20 cm) long, with a tail of another 3 inches (7.5 cm). It weighs only about 0.8 ounces (23 g). It's been around North America for a long time; scientists have found 40-million-year-old fossils of the tiny creature's ancestors!

(3)   Some people call the white-footed mouse the "wood mouse" because it lives in so many wooded areas throughout North America. Other people call the white-footed mouse the "deer mouse." One reason is that its fur is the same colors as a deer's—soft brown on its back; white on its underside. Another reason is that the mice carry deer ticks that spread Lyme disease.

(4)   The whitefoot makes its nest almost anywhere. It likes a home that is warm and dry, like a hollow tree or empty bird's nest. But most of the time the whitefoot runs along the ground looking for food. It eats seeds, nuts, leaves, bark, and insects. It sleeps by day and looks for food at night—its long whiskers and big ears help it find its way in the dark.

(5)   Does the whitefoot really make music? In a way, it does because it often makes a humming sound. And it taps its little paws very fast on a dead leaf or hollow log to make a buzzing, drumming sound! Scientists aren't sure why the mouse is a drummer; it just is!

(6)   So the next time you're in the woods, walk quietly. There might be a white-footed mouse nearby, and you wouldn't want to interrupt a mouse in the middle of its song . . . would you?

1. What is the main idea of this selection?
   a. Deer are brown and white.
   b. The white-footed mouse taps its paws in a drumming sound.
   c. The woods of North America are full of mice.
   d. Scientists study the habits of mice.

2. Which is a supporting detail for that main idea?
   a. The white-footed mouse is also known as the wood mouse.
   b. The deer mouse may carry ticks that transmit a disease.
   c. The mouse taps on a dead leaf or hollow log.
   d. The white-footed mouse isn't very big.

3. Which would make the best substitute title for this selection?
   a. "How to Build a Better Mousetrap"
   b. "Concert in the Woods"
   c. "Caution: Lyme Disease Ahead!"
   d. "All about Rodents"

4. What is the main idea of paragraph 2?
   a. The white-footed mouse lives in Canada.
   b. The white-footed mouse is also called the wood or deer mouse.
   c. The white-footed mouse hums.
   d. The white-footed mouse is very small.

5. Which detail in paragraph 2 is interesting, but not needed to find the main idea of that paragraph?
   a. Its tail is 3 inches (7.5 cm) long.
   b. Scientists found 40-million-year-old fossils of its ancestors.
   c. It weighs 0.8 ounces (23 g).
   d. Its body is about 8 inches (20 cm) long.

PRACTICE 2: DIETARY DETAILS

Read the selection, andthen answer the questions that follow.

(1) Everyone needs food as fuel for his or her body. But kids especially need the right fuel to keep their bodies going as they're growing. To help everyone figure out which foods supply the energy needed, the U.S. Department of Agriculture (USDA) developed a new Food Guide Pyramid in 2005. Look at the visual.

(2) You probably remember the old pyramid, with horizontal layers of blocks like the ancient pyramids. Well, this new pyramid has six, tall, vertical stripes instead. Each stripe represents one source of nutrition. There are horizontal steps on the side of the pyramid, but they signify the need for exercise as well as good food—30 minutes of exercise a day—to create a healthy you!

(3) This new pyramid is called MyPyramid, because it's supposed to help meet the needs of each individual. Your food needs are based on your age, if you're a girl or boy, and how active you are. You can go to the USDA website at http://mypyramid.gov to check out how much and which kinds of food you need.

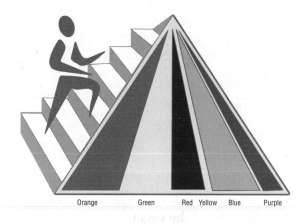

Orange   Green   Red   Yellow   Blue   Purple

(4)   Each stripe on MyPyramid is a different color:

> **Orange:** *grains*   The average kid needs 6 ounces a day from this group, which includes breads, cereals, rice, and pasta.

> **Green:** *vegetables*   The average kid needs about $2\frac{1}{2}$ cups a day from this group, which includes dark green veggies, like spinach and broccoli, and bright orange ones, like carrots.

> **Red:** *fruits*   The average kid needs about $1\frac{1}{2}$ cups of fresh, frozen, canned, or dried fruit a day.

> **Yellow:** *oils*   Kids need about 5 teaspoons of oil a day. Some have no cholesterol or are lower in fat than others. Check food labels for information.

> **Blue:** *milk*   The average kid needs about 3 cups a day of milk, yogurt, or cheese.

> **Purple:** *meat, fish, beans, and nuts*   The average kid needs about 5 ounces a day from this group.

(5)   These provide a "healthy diet." That's one that has enough of each essential nutrient; a variety from all food groups; energy to maintain a healthy weight; and no excess fat, sugar, or salt. Eating healthy and exercising daily can help reduce the risk of getting diabetes, cancer, or bone problems as you get older.

6. Which is the most likely main idea of this selection?
   a. People need to exercise at least once a week.
   b. Beans are a good source of vitamins.
   c. People need to eat a variety of good foods and exercise for a healthy life.
   d. Fiber is an important part of a healthy lifestyle.

7. Which is NOT a supporting detail for the main idea?
   a. Always use sunscreen as protection from the sun's harmful rays.
   b. Pick a variety of things from the vegetable group.
   c. Get at least a half-hour of exercise every day.
   d. Don't just pick foods from one food group.

8. Why was it suggested that someone go to the USDA website?
    a. to check the local weather
    b. to write a letter to Congress
    c. to exchange recipes for wholesome, healthy foods that taste good
    d. to find out exactly which foods and how much that individual should eat

9. Which would best be another title for the article?
    a. The Nutrition Needs of Prehistoric Humans
    b. Food for Thought
    c. The Eating Habits of Senior Citizens
    d. Thoughts about Work Routines

10. Which is the main idea of the last paragraph?
    a. It's nice to choose a variety of foods.
    b. Many older people have heart problems.
    c. Eating right and exercising now can reduce health risks in the future.
    d. Getting enough sleep is important to good health.

PRACTICE 3: RADIO DAYS

Read the selection, and then answer the questions that follow.

(1)   Before there was TV, Americans gathered around their radios daily to listen to the news and more. In the 1930s and 1940s, mystery shows, like *Sam Spade* and *The Shadow*, were favorites with young and old alike. Every week people tuned in to hear the top tunes on *Your Hit Parade*. And on Sunday mornings, radio stars read the comics aloud to kids.

(2)   Did you think soap operas were a TV phenomenon? No way! They started on radio. Do you know why they were called "soap operas"? Most shows were sponsored by soap companies and, because characters had many problems, people said the stories were like operas, most of which don't have happy endings!

(3)   Because there were no pictures to show what was going on, radio required people to use their imaginations. So, as a sportscaster described the action, people had to imagine "he hits a pop fly high into the infield, the shortstop moves in . . . reaches . . . grabs it . . . throws to second . . . and he's out!" Not only did they picture it, many people cheered as if they were right there in the stadium!

11. Which best states the main idea of the article?

    a. Soap operas started on TV.

    b. Before there was TV, people listened to the radio a lot.

    c. Quite often, operas don't end happily.

    d. Top tunes were played on the radio.

12. The author says radio required people to use their imaginations because

    a. radio stars read the comics.

    b. people cheered as if they were at the stadium.

    c. *The Shadow* was a mystery show.

    d. there were no pictures to show the action.

13. Which could the author best use as another supporting detail?

    a. Television was not in many American homes until the 1950s.

    b. Many cars did not have a radio.

    c. The modern home has two or more TVs.

    d. Two-way radios were important during the war.

ANSWERS

  1. b

  2. c

  3. b

  4. d

  5. b

  6. c

  7. a

  8. d

  9. b

10. c

11. b

12. d

13. a

chronological order

Begin at the beginning and go on till you
come to the end: then stop.
LEWIS CARROLL (1832–1898)
ENGLISH AUTHOR, *ALICE'S ADVENTURES IN WONDERLAND*

In this lesson, you'll discover that some authors write about things in the order in which they happened.

JUST EXACTLY WHAT does the word *chronological* mean? It helps to know that the Greek root *chron* means "time" and *logical* means "valid or true." So *chronological* means "in true time order" or sequence.

We do everything in sequence, one step at a time. First, you wear your clothes, then you wash them, dry them, fold them or hang them up, and put them away. Authors often use words like *first, second, next, last, before, after, then, now, later, or finally* as signals that the events in a story are being told in sequence.

Example

Before the concert, we were excited because we had awesome front row seats. Then the show began, and for awhile, it was great. But soon I couldn't even hear the music over the screams of the audience! After the concert, when we could hear again, we had pizza and listened to some *quiet* rock!

But sometimes the author doesn't use signal words, and readers must figure out the sequence from details in the text.

Example

I'm so glad to be home now, where it's quiet! Yesterday I went to a concert and it was unbelievable . . . not in a good way. The music and the crowd were so-o-o loud! At the beginning, I thought I was lucky because I got front row seats. Boy was I wrong!

The sequence of getting front row seats for a concert, suffering through the loudness of music and concertgoers, and coming home are the same, but they aren't spelled out in step-by-step order. The ability to recognize chronological order can help you understand what you read. A sequence chain can help you organize the events in a selection and help you remember what you read.

---

get front row seats → go to concert → music and crowd loud → go home to quiet

---

Besides using time order, an author may sequence things by ranking them in order of importance, speed, size, age, and so on.

PRACTICE 1: MAKE-A-MUMMY

Read the selection, and then answer the questions that follow.

(1)   At the museum today, we saw an ancient Egyptian mummy and watched a mummy-making video. You know, a mummy isn't like those scary things you see in horror movies; it's just a dead body that was treated so it wouldn't rot away!

(2)   The Egyptians were experts at wrapping their dead for the trip to the afterlife! That's what the people called the "place" they'd go after they died, where they believed they'd enjoy pretty much all the comforts of life. So, they figured it was important to keep their bodies preserved for future use!

(3)   Making a mummy was no easy job. It took about 70 days! Only special people were allowed to carry out the process. First, they cleaned the body. Then they removed most of the internal organs, including the brain. They pulled that out with a long hooked instrument inserted through the dead person's nose! The Egyptians didn't think the brain was important, so they threw it away. The lungs, stomach, and most other organs were removed through slits in the skin, then placed in special containers, called canopic jars, and buried with the mummy. Because the Egyptians believed the heart was the center of intelligence, only it was left inside the body.

Next, the body was stuffed and covered with salt to slowly suck out all the fluid. After 40 days, the shrunken body was rubbed with lotion to soften the skin. Then the body was wrapped in up to 20 layers of linen.

(4)   Gooey tree sap was spread on the linen to make the layers stick together. The workers placed a mask on the face that looked pretty much like the dead person. That was to help the person's spirit recognize him or her in the afterlife and reenter the body.

(5)   Then, one last layer of tree sap and cloth was added and it was a mummy. Finally, it was ready to be put into a stone coffin and placed in a burial chamber, along with clothing, food, furniture, toys, jewelry, and any other things it might need in the afterlife.

(6)   The mummy we saw was about 3,000 years old. I wonder if its heart is still in there?

1. What was the first thing the narrator said?
   a. "Making a mummy was no easy job."
   b. "The Egyptians didn't think the brain was important. . . ."
   c. "At the museum today, we saw an ancient Egyptian mummy. . . ."
   d. "The Egyptians were experts at wrapping their dead. . . ."

2. What was the first thing mummy-makers did to a body?
   a. pulled out the brain through the nose
   b. wrapped 20 layers of cloth around it
   c. put a mask on its face
   d. cleaned it

3. For 40 days, the body
   a. was put into a stone coffin.
   b. was covered with salt that sucked out any body fluid.
   c. was on view at a funeral home.
   d. was wrapped in a single layer of silk.

4. After 40 days, the mummy-makers
   a. took off the layers of lines.
   b. made cuts and took out the stomach.
   c. rubbed the body to soften its shrunken skin.
   d. put the brain back inside the body.

5. When was the mask put on the mummy's face?
   a. before wrapping the body in one last layer of cloth
   b. after the body was put into the coffin
   c. before the heart was removed
   d. after the burial chamber was closed

PRACTICE 2: GET ON TRACK!

Read the selection, and then answer the questions that follow.

SPEED STATISTICS	
Horse	43 mph (70 km/h)
Steam train	61 mph (98 km/h)
Diesel train	149 mph (238 km/h)
Electric train	152 mph (245 km/h)
Maglev	361 mph (581 km/h)

(1) In ancient times, humans walked to get where they wanted to go. Later, they rode domesticated animals, like camels, horses, and mules. People had to carry their belongings themselves or on an animal's back. Later, people dragged objects on a travois, a kind of platform tied between two long poles. Then came the discovery of the wheel, and new technology changed everything.

(2) People rode and carried goods in carts and wagons pulled by animals. The larger the wagon and the more animals, the more people and goods could be moved. By 1662, the first horse-drawn buses were running regular routes through busy city streets.

In 1814, the first steam-powered engine was fired up. Soon trains burned wood or coal to create steam that put the wheels in motion, rolling along tracks laid on the ground to create a "road" from place to place. The powerful engines pulled many cars full of people and goods. One engine did the work faster than a team of horses, so people called the machine the "Iron Horse."

(3) Steam trains were crucial to the growth of America. People moved west and built towns near the train tracks. Railroad owners became rich as more people traveled and shipped goods by rail. Soon hundreds of locomotives chugged across America, spewing out clouds of thick, black smoke.

(4)   In 1918, a train was first powered by a diesel engine, which produces electricity to move a train. Diesels were faster and more powerful, and they didn't pollute the air. Before long, most steam engines were replaced by diesels. Next came even faster, quieter electric trains that were powered by overhead cables or electrified rails. Those led to the growth of commuter and subway trains that are still used by millions every day.

(5)   By the 1960s, there were new high-speed, electric trains, called "bullet trains" because of their shape and speed. They were the fastest until the 1980s, when the maglev, or "magnetic levitation" train, was introduced. It doesn't run on rails; it floats between them! Electromagnets imbedded in the train and the track repel, lifting the train and pushing it forward. Today maglevs continue to get faster and faster. Right now the Japanese maglev holds the speed record, 361 mph (581 km/h)!

6. Before the discovery of the wheel, how did people travel?
   a. on foot
   b. riding camels
   c. riding mules
   d. all of the above

7. According to the article, by 1662 some cities had
   a. subways.
   b. steam trains.
   c. horse-drawn buses.
   d. commuter trains.

8. Steam trains were probably important to America in the 1800s because
   a. they made the sky dark with smoke.
   b. people moved west and built new cities that helped the country grow.
   c. they used wood or coal.
   d. people could tell time by a train's schedule.

9. Most steam engines were replaced by diesels that
   a. produced electricity to power the train.
   b. were not as powerful.
   c. produced even more smoke pollution.
   d. were first available in 1603.

10. Which was invented first?
   a. the diesel engine
   b. the bullet train
   c. the maglev
   d. the travois

11. The chart lists train engine types in sequence by
   a. importance.
   b. year invented.
   c. speed.
   d. size.

PRACTICE 3: TIME ORDER FOR FUN!

Sometimes you have to choose what you can do based on a sequence of events and what can be done at those times. Check out this camp schedule of activities, and then use the information to answer the questions and make a schedule.

CAMP SCHEDULE

8:00 A.M. Buses arrive
8:30 A.M.–12:30 P.M. Activities
12:30–1:00 P.M. Lunch is available.
1:00–1:30 P.M. Lunch is available.
1:30–4:00 P.M. Activities
4:15 P.M. Buses leave.

Acting	Gymnastics
9:00–10:00 A.M.	8:30–9:30 A.M.
11:00–noon	10:00–11:00 A.M.
12:30–1:30 P.M.	noon–1:00 P.M.
1:30–2:30 P.M.	1:30–2:30 P.M.
3:00–4:00 P.M.	3:00–4:00 P.M.

Boating	Horseback Riding
9:00–10:30 A.M.	8:30–10:30 A.M.
11:00 A.M.–12:30 P.M.	10:30 A.M.–12:30 P.M.
2:00–3:30 P.M.	1:00–3:00 P.M.
Crafts	2:00–3:00 P.M.
8:30–9:30 A.M.	**Swimming**
9:30–10:30 A.M.	9:00–11:00 A.M.
10:30–11:30 A.M.	11:00 A.M.–1:00 P.M.
2:30–3:30 P.M.	2:00–4:00 P.M.

12. A day for campers, from arrival to departure, is
   a. 7 hours and 15 minutes.
   b. 8 hours and 15 minutes.
   c. 6 hours and 30 minutes.
   d. 6 hours and 15 minutes.

13. Which are the first activities available in the morning?
   a. acting and boating
   b. swimming and crafts
   c. crafts and gymnastics
   d. gymnastics and horseback riding

14. Make a schedule that allows you to take acting, gymnastics, and boating *or* horseback riding, crafts, and swimming . . . still have lunch, and time to just hang with friends!

_____

_____

_____

ANSWERS

1. c
2. d
3. b
4. c
5. a
6. d
7. c
8. b
9. a
10. d
11. c
12. b
13. c
14. There are several possible answers; here are two: Gym 8:30–9:30, Acting 11–12, Lunch 12:30–1, Boating 2–3:30; Crafts 8:30–9:30, Swimming 11–1, Lunch 1–1:30, Horseback Riding 2–4.

cause and effect

*All science is concerned with
the relationship of cause and effect.
Each scientific discovery increases man's ability to
predict the consequences of his actions
and thus his ability to control future events.*
LAWRENCE J. PETERS (1919–1988)
AMERICAN EDUCATOR AND WRITER

In this lesson, you'll see that because things happen in sequence, one thing often makes the next happen, and you can sometimes predict what'll happen next!

THINGS DON'T JUST happen; living things and forces make them happen. Whatever or whoever makes something happen is the cause; what happens is the effect. For example, a singer hits a very high note and a glass shatters. Vibrating sound waves are the *cause*; broken glass is the *effect*.

As you read, look for clues to what makes things happen. Authors may use words to signal a cause-and-effect text structure. Words like *because* or *since* may indicate a cause, and *so* or *therefore* indicate an effect.

Examples
I missed the bus *because* I overslept.
I overslept, *so* I missed the bus.

In the examples above, the signal words point out that oversleeping was the cause and missing the bus was the effect. But sometimes there are no signal words. Readers must figure out the cause-and-effect relationship from the text.

Example

A car drove through a huge puddle and splashed water all over me!

In this example, tires splashing water are the cause; a wet person is the effect. A cause may have more than one effect and an effect more than one cause.

Example

I was late for school because I overslept and a car splashed water on me on my way to school, so I had to go back home and change clothes!

As you read, use a cause-and-effect chart to keep track of how things or people affect others.

Cause	Effect
It rained all day.	The parade was canceled.
I didn't study.	I failed the exam.

Think about it. Couldn't you *predict* that, since it rained all day, that parade would be canceled, and if someone didn't study, he or she might fail an exam? Figuring out why something happened and thinking about what might possibly happen next gets you involved and helps you better understand what you read.

PRACTICE 1: THE MAGIC OF MERLIN

Read the selection, and then answer the questions that follow.

(1)   There are many legends about King Arthur, the Knights of the Round Table, and the wizard Merlin. Of all the characters in these tales, many people find Merlin the most fascinating, being a man of mystery and magic. It's said that Merlin could talk to the animals in the forest and predict the future for kings. But unfortunately, he wasn't able to predict his own future with the Lady of the Lake!

(2)   According to a popular legend, as Merlin walked through the forest one day, he first met the Lady of the Lake. Some say he predicted he'd find her there that day, beside the forest lake that was her home, and that's why he went there. The Lady was believed to be a great sorceress herself, although not as great as Merlin. She was amazed by his powers and promised to love him if he would teach her his magic. The Lady of the Lake was quite beautiful, and Merlin fell under her spell, so he agreed.

(3)   Merlin began to teach the Lady of the Lake his most magical tricks. And for a while, she seemed happy. But she continually urged him to conjure up even greater magical feats. And she was constantly looking for some way to keep Merlin always at her side. She wanted to make sure that if he did come up with any new ideas, he'd have to share them with her!

(4)   One day, the Lady of the Lake asked Merlin to build her a magical castle. She wanted it to be so strong that no one and nothing could ever destroy it. And she requested Merlin to make her castle invisible. That might have seemed a tall order for some, but Merlin did his magic. He built her a fabulous castle by the lake and then used his wizard's powers to make the building invisible. Anyone traveling through the forest would see only the lake and not the Lady's beautiful, enchanted castle. Merlin even taught the Lady how she could make her castle appear or disappear to make sure that no one could get in or come out of it unless she wished!

(5)   The Lady of the Lake was very happy, for a while. Then she realized that Merlin still had the power to make her castle appear or disappear as well. That worried her. What if he left for good someday? She would no longer share all of the magic secrets he knew or would know in the future! So one day, as she and Merlin sat beneath a tree in the forest, she lulled him to sleep with a sweet song.

(6)   As Merlin slept, the Lady of the Lake walked around him nine times, chanting and weaving a magical spell. When he awoke, she led him to the castle. There she locked him in an enchanted tower, from which he was powerless to leave, but which she could visit or leave at will! She had used Merlin's own magic against him, and he never left her enchanted, imprisoning castle again.

1. Many people think Merlin is the most interesting character in King Arthur legends because
   a. he was not a knight.
   b. he was a wizard.
   c. he lived in a forest.
   d. his name had six letters.

2. What caused Merlin to walk by the lake one day?
   a. He predicted a bear was caught in a trap in the forest.
   b. He predicted it was a new path home from school.
   c. He predicted he'd meet the Lady of the Lake there.
   d. He predicted he could gather enough apples for a pie.

3. Because the Lady was so beautiful, Merlin
  a. fell under her spell.
  b. was frightened and ran away.
  c. pushed her into the water.
  d. turned her into a tree.

4. Why did the Lady want Merlin always at her side?
  a. so she could teach him all of the magic tricks she knew
  b. so the lake would always be filled with water
  c. so that her servants would be paid well
  d. so she'd always know all the magic secrets he knew

PRACTICE 2: THE PLANET CHANGES

Read the selection, and then answer the questions that follow.

(1)   Look at Earth's landscape today. Then look at it next month. See the difference? Well, maybe not. Earth is constantly changing, but some changes are slower than others. Here are a few examples of how our planet changes every day.

- Deep inside Earth is a huge pool of magma—melted rock and gas. If the pressure underground builds up, the magma moves up and out of an opening in Earth's crust. The liquid spills or explodes as lava, then flows downhill, destroying everything in its path. When the lava cools and hardens, it enlarges old land or creates new islands in the sea!
- Heavy rainfall can weaken soil and rock. If this happens on a hillside, the soil and rocks can break loose and slide all the way down. A landslide can topple trees, demolish houses, and dump soil to build up Earth's surface in a new location.
- Sometimes piles of snow loosen and quickly tumble down a mountain, picking up rocks as they go. Avalanches scrape the surface of the mountain and change it forever. The rocks and soil pushed along with the snow build up Earth's surface below, once the snow melts.
- Every year we hear of places where heavy rainfall or melted ice and snow run into rivers, causing them to overflow. The ensuing floods flow across the land, washing away rich soil and sometimes changing the path of the river itself.

- Earthquakes very quickly destroy some landforms and create others. Undersea earthquakes can cause tsunamis, or tidal waves, with water reaching as high as 50 feet (15 m). When the water reaches land, it crashes ashore and rearranges the landscape.
- Even lightning, tornadoes, and hurricanes quickly change Earth's surface. Lightning may cause forest fires that burn down trees and homes, and destroy land. Windstorms like tornadoes and hurricanes blow away soil and rip up trees, flattening or tearing away the land around them.
- As you see, nature is always changing Earth's surface somewhere. Some changes are big. Some are little. But all can be seen, if you look hard enough!

5. What causes magma to move up and out of Earth as lava?
   a. heavy rains and winds
   b. snow and ice
   c. pressure build-up underground
   d. pressure from strong wind

6. Which is an effect of an avalanche?
   a. Lava flows downhill, destroying everything in its path.
   b. Once the snow melts, rocks and soil pushed along build up Earth's surface.
   c. The water reaches land, crashes ashore, and rearranges the landscape.
   d. Forest fires burn down trees and homes, and destroy land.

7. How can windstorms change Earth's surface?
   a. by blowing away soil
   b. by ripping away trees
   c. by flattening and tearing away land around trees
   d. all of the above

8. Heavy rainfall on a hillside can cause
   a. a hurricane.
   b. an avalanche.
   c. a tsunami.
   d. a landslide.

9. When heavy rain or melting snow and ice run into a river, they can cause
  a. a flood.
  b. an earthquake.
  c. a hurricane.
  d. a tornado.

10. Which can you most likely predict?
  a. There will be an earthquake today.
  b. In five years, Earth's surface will look different than it does today.
  c. Earth's surface will always look the same.
  d. In five years, Earth's surface will look exactly as it does today.

PRACTICE 3: WE'VE GOT YOU COVERED

Read the selection, and then answer the questions that follow.

(1)   Trading was a source of great wealth to fourteenth-century merchants in Venice, Italy. Ships brought spices, silk, and other goods from Asia for merchants to sell to wealthy customers. With such expensive items, a merchant could become very rich in just a few years. But it took just one storm at sea or pirate attack to lose an entire cargo.

(2)   To lessen the risk, the merchants formed trade unions to provide protection against loss. That was the beginning of insurance. Each merchant paid a certain amount of money to be used to help any member who suffered a loss. Soon, merchants in other countries began to provide "insurance" on their goods.

(3)   The first life insurance policy was sold in England in the sixteenth century. A century later, the first fire insurance became available. And in 1752, Benjamin Franklin founded a U.S. insurance company so people didn't lose everything in a fire. Today, thousands of U.S. companies insure businesses and individuals for everything from life and fire to identity theft.

11. Venetian merchants in the fourteenth century became very wealthy because
  a. pirates attacked their ships.
  b. Benjamin Franklin sold them insurance.
  c. they sold spices, silks, and other goods from Asia to rich customers.
  d. they had life insurance.

12. Venetian merchants wanted to lessen their risk of losing goods, so
   a. they hired pirates to steal some for them.
   b. they closed their shops every Saturday
   c. they moved to America.
   d. they formed trade unions.

13. Benjamin Franklin founded a U.S. insurance company so that
   a. people could buy silk from Asia.
   b. people didn't lose everything in a fire.
   c. people could join the actor's union.
   d. people lost everything in a fire.

ANSWERS

1. b
2. c
3. a
4. d
5. c
6. b
7. d
8. d
9. a
10. b
11. c
12. d
13. b

compare and contrast

Shall I compare thee to a Summer's day?
Thou art more lovely and more temperate.
WILLIAM SHAKESPEARE (1564–1616)
ENGLISH POET AND PLAYWRIGHT

In this lesson, you'll discover that authors often describe how things are alike or different.

SOME AUTHORS USE a compare-and-contrast text structure to organize ideas. To compare, they tell how things are alike; to contrast, they tell how things are different. Words like *same, different, some, all, every, also, but, both,* or *many* signal to readers that the author is using a compare-and-contrast structure.

Compare: *Every* student in the school wore the *same* blue uniform.

Contrast: They may have to wear uniforms, *but* we don't!

Authors don't always use signal words. Then, readers must figure out what's being compared or contrasted.

Example
The DJ played classic rock and everyone agreed the music was cool . . . or as some put it, "fierce!" How could I tell my new friends that I preferred country-western?

Many times things can be alike in one or more ways but still be different. In the preceding example, rock and country-western are alike because both are kinds of music, but they are different in style and rhythm. A Venn diagram can help you keep track of likenesses and differences as you read.

Example

Marissa and Matthew are twins, but she has dark hair and he's a blond. Everyone in their family has brown eyes. Matthew plays drums and Marissa plays guitar in the school band. They both sing and want to start a rock group.

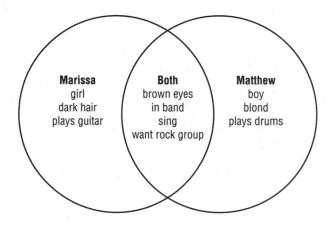

PRACTICE 1: *THE CITY MOUSE AND THE COUNTRY MOUSE*

An Aesop's Fable Retold

Read the selection, and then answer the questions that follow.

(1) Once there were two mouse cousins. One lived in the country; the other lived in a big city. They wrote to each other often and invited each other to visit.

(2) "You must come to see how nice it is in the city," wrote the City Mouse. "I have a choice of wonderful foods to eat every day, like bread, cheese, and sweets. What do you eat?"

(3) "I eat seeds from the fields," the Country Mouse wrote back. "And I sometimes find crumbs in the old farmhouse where I live."

(4) One day, as the Country Mouse hunted for grain in the field, he thought of his cousin choosing what to eat. "Why should I have to hunt for food?" he said to no one at all. "I think I will head to this city my cousin keeps telling me about!"

(5) And so he did. When the Country Mouse arrived, the City Mouse said, "Shhh! The people just left the dining room. Let's sneak in for some bread and cheese."

(6) The Country Mouse was amazed at the leftover food just sitting on a table. "Dig in!" said the City Mouse, and he bit into a chunk of cheese.

(7) The Country Mouse took a nibble. He'd never tasted anything so delicious! He was thinking how lucky the City Mouse was when he heard a noise. "Run!" said the City Mouse, as he grabbed his cousin's paw. "Someone's come to clean off the table!"

(8) The two mice ran to a little hole in the kitchen wall. Inside, the Country Mouse trembled as someone stacked dishes in a dishwasher and went away. The City Mouse smiled, "Good, he didn't see us. Let's go get something else."

(9) The Country Mouse looked around. He'd never seen so many jars and bags and boxes! "What luck!" said the City Mouse. "Someone left the cookies open!"

(10) The cousins climbed to a shelf where a cookie bag sat. After much pulling and tugging, they got a large chunk of oatmeal cookie out and began to nibble on it. Suddenly, the Country Mouse heard a loud MEOW! "Run!" cried the City Mouse. And they ran as fast as they could, back to the hole in the wall.

(11) The City Mouse laughed as the Country Mouse shook with fear. "Don't be so scared, Cousin; it's only the cat! True, she likes to eat mice and she has sharp claws, but she'll go away in a few minutes. Then we can go eat more food!"

(12) The Country Mouse shook his head. "No, thanks, Cousin. I'm going home! Thank you for your hospitality, but I would rather eat my lowly grain and crumbs in safety than have your fine menu and be in danger all the time!"

(13) And so the Country Mouse went home and happily ate in peace the rest of his days.

1. How are the City Mouse and the Country Mouse alike?
   a. Each has a cousin.
   b. Each likes cheese.
   c. Both are mice.
   d. all of the above

2. From the text, you know that one difference between the two mice is
   a. that the City Mouse is taller.
   b. when each one was born.
   c. where each one lives.
   d. that the Country Mouse can't read.

3. The City Mouse and the Country Mouse are alike because
   a. each spends money on food.
   b. each is a boy.
   c. each likes dogs.
   d. each is a girl.

4. The Country Mouse went back home because he thought
   a. he could teach the farmer to make cheese.
   b. he would be fired from his computer job.
   c. he had forgotten to lock the farmhouse door.
   d. he would be safer eating crumbs there than having treats in the city.

PRACTICE 2: SNOW CAT

Read the selection, and then answer the questions that follow.

(1)   The snow leopard lives in the rocky mountain caves of Central Asia, some 6,000–18,000 feet (1,829–5,486 m) above sea level. The animal's beautiful, soft, gray fur is speckled with black or brown ringed spots. Its thick tail, which is more than $\frac{1}{3}$ of its 6–7.5 foot (2–2.3 m) total length, is heavy with fur to protect the animal from extreme cold. The snow leopard uses its tail both for balance and to wrap around its curled-up body and cover its nose and mouth in subzero temperatures. The bottoms of its large, furry paws are also covered with fur to help protect the pads from the cold, sharp ice and jagged rocks.

(2)   The snow leopard is like other big cats in some ways and different in others. For example, other big cats roar, but not the snow leopard. It purrs like many smaller cats! And the snow leopard feeds in a crouched position, like a house cat, instead of lying down like other big cats. Most leopards hunt at night, often leaping from trees to chase down their prey, then store the food high in a tree away from other predators. But snow leopards hunt in the early morning and late afternoon. They rest on cliff edges, waiting for prey to pass by. Then the cat may leap as much as 50 feet uphill to capture a meal.

(3)   Prey consists of almost any available animal, like wild sheep, goats, deer, or birds. Then, since there are no trees high in the mountains to store food in, the snow leopard stays on the ground close to its kill, often returning for three or four days to feed.

(4)   In spring, a female snow leopard has from one to four kittens. They stay with their mothers through their first winter, then go off to hunt on their own.

(5)   Snow leopards are extremely rare; in fact they're an endangered species. Many have been hunted for their beautiful fur and their bones, which are ground up and used in some Chinese medicines. Scientists estimate there are only about 4,000–7,000 snow leopards left in the wild. You may be able to see one in a zoo. There are 600–700 snow leopards living safely in zoos around the world.

5. According to the article, the snow leopard is like a small cat because
   a. it lives in the mountains.
   b. it eats in a crouched position.
   c. it hunts at night.
   d. it roars.

6. A snow leopard is like all other leopards because
   a. it is a member of the cat family.
   b. it has fur.
   c. it has four feet.
   d. all of the above

7. A snow leopard is different from other leopards because
   a. it is a predator.
   b. it has kittens.
   c. it hunts in the daytime.
   d. it eats meat.

8. The snow leopard doesn't store its food in trees because
   a. there are no trees high in the mountains.
   b. it can't climb like other leopards.
   c. the trees are full of leaves.
   d. it eats all of the prey in one meal.

9. Once there were many snow leopards, but now there are only about
   a. 2,000–3,000 in zoos and in the wild.
   b. 4,000–5,000 in zoos.
   c. 4,000–7,000 in the wild.
   d. 6,000–8,000 living.

10. Which do both snow leopards and other leopards do when they hunt?
   a. roar
   b. leap
   c. sing
   d. sleep

PRACTICE 3: STONE STRUCTURES

Read the selection, and then answer the questions that follow.

(1)   Ancient people built rock monuments, many of which are still standing. Stonehenge was built in England about 5,000 years ago. Its rocks were arranged in four circles, with 30 large rocks on the outsides, some of which weighed 40 tons! It's believed that people may have used Stonehenge to predict the seasons.

(2)   About 4,500 years ago, the Egyptians used millions of stone blocks to build pyramids as tombs for their kings. Pyramids, of course, are pointed at the top. The Egyptians believed the pointed tombs helped their rulers get to heaven.

(3)   The Great Wall of China was built more than 2,000 years ago. The 1,200-mile- (1,900-km-) long rock structure was created to keep invaders out of China. Today, tourists take long walks along the top of the winding wall.

(4)   On Easter Island, off the coast of Chile, stand giant rock statues with large heads and thick bodies. About 600, measuring up to 60 feet (18 m) tall, were created more than 1,000 years ago. Today only about 100 are left. It's believed that islanders may have carved them as monuments to their ancestors.

11. How are all the monuments alike?
  a. All are in Europe.
  b. All have faces.
  c. All are made of rock.
  d. All were put in place by giant bulldozers.

12. One difference between the pyramids and the Easter Island rocks is that
  a. the Easter Island statues are set up in four circles.
  b. the pyramids are tombs for kings, and the statues are not.
  c. the Easter Island statues were built long ago.
  d. some pyramids are still standing.

13. The Great Wall and Stonehenge are different because
  a. they were built in different countries at different times.
  b. both are made of rock.
  c. only the Great Wall was constructed by humans.
  d. each can still be seen today.

ANSWERS

1. d
2. c
3. b
4. d
5. b
6. d
7. c
8. a
9. c
10. b
11. d
12. b
13. a

fact and opinion

*Our opinions do not really blossom into fruition until we have
expressed them to someone else.*

Mark Twain [Samuel Clemens] (1835–1910)
American writer, humorist

In this lesson, you'll discover how facts and opinions are used to persuade you
to do something.

A **FACT IS** a detail that can be proven true. An **opinion** is what someone thinks,
it can't be proven true or false.

Fact	Opinion
The Harry Potter books were written by J.K. Rowling.	The third Harry Potter book was the best.
Corn is a vegetable.	Corn tastes better than carrots.
Painting is an art.	Da Vinci was the world's greatest painter.
Spring is one of the four seasons.	Spring is the best season of the year.

You can prove each fact is true. Just look it up in a book or on the Internet. But
other people may have different ideas about the Harry Potter books, carrots versus corn, the greatest painter, and the best season!

Authors use facts and opinions to persuade you to think or do something. The author states an idea, and then gives details to convince you to
agree. Details may be facts, dates, statistics, or words that affect your feelings.
Only you can decide if the evidence is strong enough to convince you. Commercials and print ads are familiar forms of persuasive writing.

Kind	How it's done	Example
Bandwagon	makes you think everyone does it, so you should, too	GloryFoot boots are the hottest new fashion! Don't be left out, get yours today!
Expert Opinion	quotes someone who's an expert in the field	"I hike up a lot of hot volcanoes," says Dr. E. Ruption, "so I'm glad to have Frosty-Foot slippers to slide into after work!"
Glittering Generalities	appeal to emotions, like patriotism, success, family	Vote for A. Ballot . . . the candidate to ensure the safety of your family and our nation!
Name Calling	uses rude or mocking language with negative connotations	Switch from greasy, heart-clogging Acme-Burgers to Pine-Burgers, the healthy fiber-filled food that's better for your body!
Personal Experience	explains how the author came to this belief	I have been in Africa and seen so many children who need our help.
Testimonial	quotes a famous person who supports the idea	"We must all do what we can to help the penguins," said superathlete Ima Star, who donated $10,000. How will you help?

The more aware you become of persuasive techniques, the better you can evaluate the truth of what you read. And the better you can "see through" things you hear or see in real-life situations.

PRACTICE 1: ENVIRONMENTAL EMERGENCY!

Read the speech, and then answer the questions that follow.

(1) Ladies and Gentlemen, thank you for coming. When I first heard about the state's plan to build an oil storage facility and recycling plant near White River, I thought of the weekends my family spent there every summer when I was a kid. We'd camp out and fish, swim, and explore caves in the nearby woods. My grandfather taught me how to fish there. And he and I spent hours hiking in the woods, where I learned to identify local plants and animals.

(2)   The river and the land around it were both familiar and unique. I learned a lot there from my grandfather, and today, I'm a grandfather. I take my grandchildren there, but it's changed. There aren't as many fish, and some animals no longer inhabit the woods. According to Dr. Ima Expert, that's because "they find it difficult to adjust to constant noise from new highways and to avoid dangers from trash left by careless hikers." My grandkids and I usually spend at least one weekend each summer cleaning up after folks who recklessly leave plastic materials that harm animals.

(3)   Now, we face the danger of losing more animals from possible oil spills at the proposed facility! Our river and the animals need to be protected and preserved. The danger is real, and only we, the people, can stop it. If we allow our rich natural resources to be destroyed, our lives will be forever changed. We won't be able to undo what we have done. These new facilities will discharge waste into the river. That will impact not only our part of the river but all of it as it travels toward the ocean. Animals and nearby soil will become contaminated.

(4)   We must protect our environment. So I ask each of you to join us in trying to stop the project. Please write, call, or e-mail local elected officials, and federal officials, to register your concerns. And if you really care about the environment, please join us next Saturday in a protest march to the state capital. Leading us will be TV star Mark MiWords. He grew up around here and says, "We must make sure that our grandchildren's grandchildren will be able to share the same experiences we had on the river as kids." Please, join us. Thank you.

1. What does the author of this speech want people to do?
    a. help to stop the building of a new middle school
    b. help to raise money to restock the river with fish
    c. help to stop the building of oil and recycling plants by the river
    d. help to raise money to build oil and recycling plants by the river

2. Which of these does the author NOT use?
    a. expert opinion
    b. testimonial
    c. glittering generalities
    d. name calling

3. Which of these is NOT an opinion?
   a. The plant will ruin the environment forever.
   b. The state has plans to build an oil storage plant.
   c. If you care about the environment, you'll join our cause.
   d. Mark MiWords is a really great actor.

4. Which of these is an opinion and cannot be proved true?
   a. Oil can pollute water.
   b. There are less fish in White River today.
   c. You can have hours of fun by the river.
   d. There is a highway close to the forest.

5. How does the author use personal experiences to influence people? Use at least three examples from the speech.

   _____

   _____

   _____

PRACTICE 2: LIGHTS! CAMERA! ACTION!

Read these two commercials, and then answer the questions that follow.

Commercial 1: Right-Here Notebooks

Reports . . . homework . . . class notes . . . lists of things to do! Keeping all those papers neat wasn't always easy. That's why I bought this RIGHT-HERE organizer. *(open)* Look . . . no more messy, wrinkled, crinkled, crumpled papers *(pause)* and no more Mr. Ferro yelling at me for handing in ripped and "very untidy" work! Now everything's neat and in its place *(looks inside)* Oh, no . . . where's my math homework? *(pause, then smile)* That's right . . . I'm getting so efficient I handed it in already! Get a RIGHT-HERE today. . . . It'll get you organized so you get better grades!

Commercial 2: Acting Studio

[*Teen and younger child watching TV movie. Younger child screams.*]

TEEN: Oh . . . don't be such a baby!!

CHILD: But the guy got hurt!

TEEN: It's just make-believe!

CHILD: Well, how do they get so good at it?

TEEN: They go to acting school.

CHILD: So . . . if I go to acting school . . . I'll be in a movie?

TEEN: No, silly, then you need an agent . . . then you need to audition! If they like what you do, then, yes, you'll be in a movie . . . *but* first, get acting lessons.

CHILD: I want to do it!

TEEN: Well, ask Mom about taking lessons at Dance-'n'-Arts.

CHILD: Really? They have acting lessons there?

TEEN: Yeah . . . really!

CHILD: [*Calls off-stage*] MOM!!

ANNOUNCER [*Voice-Over*]: Sign your child up today! Call 555-6070 . . . classes start soon!

6. What does the author of Commercial 1 want TV viewers to do?
   a. watch a certain TV show
   b. join a swimming club
   c. buy a certain notebook
   d. do more homework

7. Which does the author use in Commercial 1 use in the last sentence?
   a. expert opinion
   b. glittering generality
   c. bandwagon
   d. name calling

8. What does the author of Commercial 2 want TV viewers to do?
   a. help save the library
   b. teach in the local schools
   c. build an acting school
   d. take acting lessons

9. How can viewers find out if the last line of Commercial 2 is a fact or an opinion?
  a. Watch the commercial again.
  b. Write a fan letter to the teen actor.
  c. Call the number and ask.
  d. Draw a picture of the ad and see if it makes sense.

10. Imagine the teen actor in Commercial 2 was famous and said: "**I** studied there, and now I've got my own TV show!" Which would the commercial be using?
  a. testimonial
  b. glittering generality
  c. bandwagon
  d. expert opinion

PRACTICE 3: THE BILL OF RIGHTS

Read the selection, and then answer the questions that follow.

(1)   In 1787, the U.S. Constitution was written. It spelled out how the new country should be run. But before it could become the law of the land, it had to be sent to each of the 13 original states for ratification, or acceptance. Many states ratified only when they were promised that a bill of rights would be added.

(2)   The first Congress met in 1789 to write amendments, or additions, to the Constitution. The first ten amendments, called the Bill of Rights, guaranteed rights, or freedoms, the colonists had fought for in the Revolutionary War. Freedom: of worship, of speech, to hold peaceful meetings, to request the government to change unfair laws, and to bear arms. The Bill also affirmed that: A person was innocent until proven guilty, law officers couldn't enter a home without a warrant, and an accused person had a right to a trial by jury.

(3)   Before the Bill could be officially added to the Constitution, it had to be ratified by three-fourths of the 13 states. It was, in 1791. But Georgia, Massachusetts, and Connecticut didn't ratify until 1939 . . . 148 years later! It was about time!

11. Which of the following is NOT a fact because it can't be proved?
    a. The Bill of Rights affirms a citizen's right to freedom of speech.
    b. The Constitution was written in 1787.
    c. The Bill of Rights affirms a citizen's right to grow long hair.
    d. The first Congress met in 1789.

12. Which of the following is an opinion?
    a. The Constitution is a set of rules for running America.
    b. Congress wrote the amendments called the Bill of Rights.
    c. Freedom of speech is guaranteed by the Bill of Rights.
    d. All of the 13 states should have ratified the Bill of Rights in 1791!

13. How could you find out if the statement about some states not ratifying for 148 years is a fact or an opinion?
    a. Ask a friend if it makes sense.
    b. Research in a history book or on the Internet.
    c. Listen to music from the 1700s.
    d. Take a survey in class.

ANSWERS

1. c
2. d
3. b
4. c
5. Some examples: fishing with his grandfather, hiking with the grandfather, taking his own grandchildren there
6. c
7. b
8. d
9. c
10. a
11. c
12. d
13. b

LESSON 18

question and answer

Judge a man by his questions rather than by his answers.

VOLTAIRE (1694–1778)
FRENCH WRITER AND PHILOSOPHER

In this lesson, you'll find out how authors ask you questions to keep you interested in what they write!

SOME AUTHORS USE a question-and-answer text structure. This text structure is especially common in science books. The author asks readers a question, then answers it. Sometimes the answer can easily be found in the text word for word.

Example
What lets you see tiny things up close and personal? A microscope! It gives you a peek at a tiny world that plays a big part in our lives!

Other times, readers have to put details from the text together to get the answer.

Example
How does a microscope work? Light reflects off objects and bends as it goes through a lens. When the light reaches your eyes, the objects look larger than they are.

And other times, an author wants to connect with readers . . . to get them involved. So the author asks a personal question.

Example

Do you use a microscope in science class? Then you know how tiny things look bigger.

Words like *who, what, when, where, why,* and *how* signal readers that an author is using a question-and-answer text structure. A question mark can also be a signal, but sometimes the author's question is not stated directly.

Example

People wonder how big a microscope can make things look. Well, the first ones made things 10 times larger. Now microscopes make things 2,000 times larger. And electron microscopes reflect electric particles instead of light off objects to make things 200,000 times larger!

Use a question-and-answer chart to keep track of what's asked and answered.

Question	Answer
What lets you see tiny things?	a microscope
How does a microscope work?	light rays bend through the lens and make things look bigger to the eye
How big can a microscope make things?	first up to 10 times bigger; today regular 2,000 times; electronic ones 200,000 times bigger

PRACTICE 1: ANIMAL ACTION

Read the selection, and then answer the questions that follow.

(1)   What was the first domesticated, or trained, animal? Archaeologists have found evidence of trained dogs as far back as 15,000 years ago! That would make them the first species to be domesticated by humans.

Four-Footed Workforce

(2)   What did humans train dogs to do? Prehistoric hunters first trained dogs to hunt big prey. Later, Egyptian pharaohs also used dogs for hunting. In ancient Rome, dogs not only hunted, but performed in circuses and went to war.

(3)   Most commonly, dogs were used to guard important buildings, army bases, and the homes of the wealthy. Dogs also herded sheep and other farm animals, and some canines used their sensitive noses to search for lost or injured humans. Other dogs pulled small carts or sleds filled with people or goods.

(4)   There are still many working dogs today. They still hunt, guard, search for and rescue humans, and pull sleds. They also help handicapped humans. Trained dogs guide people who can't see, can't hear, or are wheelchair bound.

Moving In

(5)   So is work the only thing in a dog's life? No! Over the centuries, dogs became pets. After years of living outdoors, they weren't just allowed inside; they were welcomed as members of the family!

(6)   In the nineteenth century, England held the first dog show. Today many dog shows are held around the world so people can proudly parade their pampered pets. Are dogs the most popular pet? In America, they were until the 1990s. Then cats clawed and purred their way to the top as the most popular pet!

1. What does the author's first question ask?
   a. What did archaeologists find?
   b. Where were the fossils of the first trained animal found?
   c. What animal was the first to be domesticated?
   d. Who first trained lions and other big cats?

2. The ancient Romans used domesticated dogs to
   a. control herds of dinosaurs.
   b. hunt, perform in circuses, help in war.
   c. dive for pearls.
   d. haul rock for the building of the pyramids.

3. The word *canines* in the article is a synonym for
   a. cats.
   b. sheep.
   c. pigs.
   d. dogs.

4. The words *dogs became pets* answer which of the author's questions?
  a. Are wolves a dog's ancestors?
  b. What did humans train dogs to do?
  c. Is work the only thing in a dog's life?
  d. Why can some dogs follow a scent better than others?

5. In the United States today,
  a. cats are the most popular pets.
  b. dogs are the most popular pets.
  c. cats and dogs can never get along.
  d. dogs can't be used in movies.

6. What is the answer to the author's second question: *What did humans train dogs to do?* Give at least four examples from the article.

_____

_____

_____

_____

PRACTICE 2: A SPEEDY EXIT

Read the selection, and then answer the questions that follow.

(1) You're sweeping a dusty floor or sliding into second base. Suddenly some dust flies up your nose, irritating and tickling the insides. What can you do? You suddenly gasp and make a strange sound . . . AH-CHOO!

(2) A rapid, violent stream of air rushes from your nose and mouth, carrying the dust with it! Out come up to 40,000 tiny liquid droplets at speeds of up to 150 mph (241 kph)! It's a sneeze. Unfortunately, that sneeze can blow out germs, too. Does that tell you why it's so important to cover your mouth when you AH- CHOO?

Reflex Reaction

(3) Can you stop a sneeze from happening? No, your body acts automatically. Sensitive nerve endings that line your nose react to the invading stuff. Quickly, they send a message to your brain for help. Your brain then relays a message to some muscles in your body, telling them to work

together to get rid of the stuff. Your stomach and chest muscles, your diaphragm (that large muscle under your lungs), your throat muscles, and even the muscles in your eyelids respond and go into action! Are you surprised to know your eyelids are involved? That's why you close their eyes when you sneeze!

(4)   Sneezing is a reflex action, over which you have no control. So some people once believed it was the closest thing to dying. According to a legend, that's why we have the tradition of saying, "Bless you" when someone sneezes. Other people believed a sneeze was a sign you'd soon come down with a serious life-threatening disease, like pneumonia or the plague! Today we know that sneezing's just a natural reaction to stuff in our environment. Even so, lots of people still remember to say, "Bless you" when anyone sneezes! In Germany, people say *gesundheit* (guh-ZUNT-hīt), a word that means "health."

Sneeze Makers

(5)   Is dust the only thing that causes a sneeze? No way. Things like pepper, cold air, animal dander, pollen, and even sunlight can trigger a sneeze. About one in three people sneezes when exposed to very bright light, like from the sun, glaring headlights, or intense camera lights.

(6)   Have you ever felt like you were going to sneeze, but it seems to get stuck? The dust or other substance in your nose continues to tickle and annoy you. You may cough. You may even gasp in a few breaths of air and stand there panting, waiting for a sneeze to burst forth. But nothing happens! You try rubbing the sides of your nose and wiggling it, thinking that may help. It doesn't! Well, if ever that happens to you, try looking briefly . . . ever so briefly . . . at a bright lightbulb. Maybe you'll unstick your sneeze!

7. To answer the author's first question, readers need to
   a. look right there in the same sentence.
   b. put together ideas from the first two paragraphs.
   c. look up the answer in a dictionary.
   d. review information from the glossary.

8. Why did the author ask the question at the end of paragraph 2?
   a. to use the word AH-CHOO again
   b. to ask readers what a nostril is
   c. to remind readers to throw away tissues
   d. to make a connection with the reader

9. The words *No, it's a reflex action* are the answer to which question?
- **a.** Can only dust cause a sneeze?
- **b.** Do your stomach muscles help you sneeze?
- **c.** Can you stop a sneeze?
- **d.** Can dust really blow up into your nose?

10. Which question might the author have added in paragraph 4?
- **a.** What is the German word for *nose*?
- **b.** In which year did millions of people die of the plague?
- **c.** Does a sneeze cause pneumonia?
- **d.** Why do we say, "Bless you"?

11. The author says you may be able to "unstick" a sneeze by
- **a.** looking at a bright light.
- **b.** standing on your head.
- **c.** jumping up and down.
- **d.** going to a hospital emergency room.

PRACTICE 3: CHAMELEONS: QUICK-CHANGE ARTISTS

Read the selection, and then answer the questions that follow.

(1)   Why do chameleons change color? Some people think it's an example of natural camouflage that lets chameleons blend into their environment. But that's not really why. They change color as an emotional reaction to life!

(2)   How does a chameleon change color? The animal's transparent outer skin separates light rays, like a prism. Underneath are two layers of cells with red and yellow specks. Under that is a cell layer that reflects blue and white light. Amounts of heat and light, and the animal's emotions, expand or contract the cells. How they line up determines the chameleon's color!

(3)   If a chameleon's frightened or angry, it turns yellow. When it's happy, it turns green. When it's cold, the animal flattens its body to capture the sun's rays, and turns brown. When it's sleeping, a chameleon turns gray. So even though it doesn't really change color as camouflage from predators, it often works that way. A happy chameleon can hide in green grass and a sun-soaking chameleon can safely hide on a brown tree trunk!

12. Which answers the author's first question?
    a. Some people think the color change is natural camouflage.
    b. They change color as an emotional response.
    c. Some change as they get older.
    d. Most change only when they are wet.

13. What is another way to ask the author's second question?
    a. What color is a chameleon's outer layer of skin?
    b. How does sound affect a chameleon?
    c. Why are some chameleons green?
    d. How do a chameleon's skin cells affect its color?

14. Which would be the *best* question for an author to ask in the last paragraph?
    a. Where do chameleons live?
    b. When does a chameleon sleep?
    c. Which color is a happy chameleon?
    d. What predators hunt for chameleons?

ANSWERS

1. c
2. b
3. d
4. c
5. a
6. There are many listed; here is one possible answer: Humans have trained dogs to hunt, herd, guard, and guide the blind.
7. b
8. d
9. c
10. d
11. a
12. b
13. d
14. c

problem and solution

The greatest challenge to any thinker is stating the problem in a way that will allow a solution.

BERTRAND RUSSELL (1872–1970)
BRITISH PHILOSOPHER AND HISTORIAN

In this lesson, you'll learn that some authors tell you about problems and how to solve them.

SOME AUTHORS USE a problem-and-solution text structure to organize their ideas. An author may state a problem, and then describe a solution.

Example

After the school fire, there was a lot of damage. Our computer lab was a total loss. So we put on a fund-raising carnival the next Saturday. We used all the money to buy new computers!

Problem: A fire ruined the school computers.
Solution: Raise money at a school carnival for new computers.

Sometimes an author tells a solution, and then states the problem it solves.

Example

We had a great fund-raising carnival last Saturday. We raised a lot of money to buy new computers. We needed them after we had a fire at the school. Our computer lab had been a total loss!

Solution: Have a fund-raising carnival.
Problem: Fire ruined school computers.

Recognizing a problem-and-solution text structure helps readers better understand the relationships between events. Try this one.

Example

"It'll be okay," our bus driver said as she closed the cell phone. "We'll have this flat tire fixed in no time. The school principal said a mechanic is on the way."

Problem: a flat tire on school bus.

Solution: school is sending mechanic.

You can use a problem-solution chart to record relationships like this.

Problem	Solution
fire damages computers	have a fund-raiser
flat tire	mechanic to fix tire

PRACTICE 1: WISDOM OF THE AGES

Read the selection, and then answer the questions that follow.

[*Jared seated, listening to music. Enter Cole*]

COLE: Hi! [*No response . . . taps Jared on shoulder*] Hi! You busy?

JARED: [*removes earphones*] I was just listening to music, why?

COLE: It's . . . I mean . . . there's like this dance at school . . . and all the guys are inviting girls.

JARED [*amazed*]: This is a problem?

COLE: I just don't know how to ask a girl to go with me!

JARED: Got somebody in mind?

COLE: Yes . . . uh, Sabrina. She's, you know, nice! But what do I say? I don't want to sound like I, you know, LIKE her! And I thought . . . you know . . . since you're so cool with girls . . .

JARED [*interrupts, a bit amazed*]: Me? Oh, yeah . . . well, cool enough, I guess! I mean, I don't get any complaints!

COLE: I know . . . so I thought you'd know what to do, since girls say you're cute and all.

JARED [*surprised*]: They do? [*with confidence*] I mean . . . of course they do! [*pause*] Has any *particular* girl said that?

COLE: That good-looking girl with the long red hair said she thought you were "all that!"

JARED [*surprised and eager*]: What girl? What's her name?

COLE [*casually*]: I can't remember . . . but anyway, lots of girls like you. Now tell me how to get just *one* girl to go to the party with me!

JARED: Okay . . . we'll get back to that redhead later. Now, about your friend. [*pause to think, proudly gets an idea*] Just casually walk up to her and say, "Hi, Sabrina! You look really great today." Talk about anything, homework or whatever, for a couple of minutes, then spring it on her!

COLE: Spring *what* on her?

JARED: Flash your brightest smile and say, "Going to the dance with anyone, Sabrina?" If she says yes, say, "Good, I'll see you there!" BUT, if she says no, say, "Oh, yes you are . . . you're going with me!" And smile!

COLE: That's good! Thanks, Jared. I knew you'd know what to do!

JARED: Now . . . back to that redhead. You don't remember her name?

COLE: I never heard it. All I know is that she's Pat Elliot's sister.

JARED: Marci Elliot? I can't believe it! She's the most popular girl in school! And she likes me? Wow! I think I'll ride my bike by her house right now!

COLE: Wait! I thought you said not to let on that you really like a girl?

JARED: When you get a little older, Cole, you'll be a little wiser . . . like me! Then you'll know when to let 'em know you like 'em . . . and when not to! [*exits, saying, "Marci Elliot, are you a lucky girl or what?"*]

1. What problem does Cole have in the play?
   a. He needs to learn how to do the mambo.
   b. He needs his brother to sign his report card.
   c. He needs to have a new suit for the school dance.
   d. He needs to ask a girl to the school dance.

2. Why does Cole think Jared can solve the problem?
   a. Jared's older and girls seem to like him.
   b. Cole knows Jared has a sister named Marci.
   c. Jared studied about girls in ancient Egypt.
   d. Cole thinks Jared likes Sabrina's mom.

3. What is Jared's main problem in the play?
   a. He has a crush on Sabrina's mom.
   b. He needs to find out the name of the red-haired girl.
   c. His MP3 player broke.
   d. His favorite shoes don't fit anymore.

4. How does Cole solve Jared's problem?
   a. He calls Sabrina to get the red-haired girl's name.
   b. He sees the red-haired girl's picture in the school yearbook.
   c. He spots the girl on TV giving the weather.
   d. He remembers that her last name is Elliot.

PRACTICE 2: THE MACHINE AGE

Read the selection, and then answer the questions that follow.

(1)   For centuries, people made by hand most of the things they needed or wanted. They built houses, bridges, other structures, clothing, and furniture from materials that nature provided. People made tools and home furnishings in their homes or small workshops. They might make an extra or two to sell. But there was a problem: Only one item could be made at a time. Then in the seventeenth and early eighteenth centuries, the Industrial Revolution changed things forever. Goods were made by mass production.

(2)   Mass production is the making of many items at one time. Rich people built large factories. Inside, workers ran machines that turned out many copies of the same product at the same time. Back when just one person made an object, he or she had to gather the parts, prepare them, and put them together. Sometimes, that meant using a different tool for each task. The production process was slow. But mass production solved that problem. Now each worker did just one task. And each task required just one tool. The whole process took less time. Factory owners made more items and sold them at lower prices.

(3)   But mass production also created a problem. Some workers were bored, doing the same job repeatedly, day after day. A few became so bored they didn't pay attention to what they were doing. They didn't feel responsible for the quality of the item because they had so little to do with the finished product. People began to complain that the quality of some items was not as good as before. That's when robots came to the rescue.

(4)   Robots are good for doing boring, repeating motions. The first industrial robot was used in 1954. It was an electronically controlled arm that lifted heavy things all day. Today robots still load and unload heavy items. But they also weld metal parts together, mix dangerous chemicals, spray paint, pack finished products, and even do guard duty! Mechanical work-

ers increase production because they work day and night, without lunch or vacation breaks! Robots do the work faster than humans do. But factories still need humans to program the computers that control the mechanical mates!

5. According to the first paragraph, why was there a problem when people made their own things by hand?
   a. There were no natural materials for building homes.
   b. Only one item could be made at a time.
   c. No one knew how to make a table.
   d. Only one person knew how to make a bridge.

6. How did the Industrial Revolution solve that problem?
   a. More natural wood resources were discovered.
   b. People discovered gold on the moon.
   c. People went back to making one thing at a time.
   d. Factories used machines for mass production.

7. Back when just one person made an object, it sometimes meant using
   a. a different tool for each task.
   b. the same tool for every task.
   c. the same material with another worker.
   d. a different color every time.

8. Which problem did mass production most likely cause?
   a. Some cities had many factories.
   b. Some workers were bored doing one thing over and over
   c. Many workers ate lunch.
   d. Many factory owners had big offices.

9. Which problem did some bored workers cause?
   a. The quality of products fell.
   b. The number of products fell.
   c. The quality of products increased.
   d. The cost of products increased.

10. How did robots solve a problem? Give at least three examples from the article.

_____

_____

_____

PRACTICE 3: A TEEN PATRIOT

Read the selection, and then answer the questions that follow.

(1) The Ludingtons lived in New York, an American colony fighting for independence from England. One rainy April night in 1777, a boy rode up shouting, "Danbury's burning!" He'd come from nearby Danbury, Connecticut. "The British have attacked the city!" he cried. "General George Washington must send troops!"

(2) Mr. Ludington led the local Minutemen—live-at-home soldiers who were ready to fight at a minute's notice. He knew they could reach Danbury long before Washington's troops. But someone had to rally his men to gather for battle. He sent his 16-year-old daughter Sybil to tell them. All night the tired, frightened girl rode. She covered 40 miles (64 km), shouting from house to house, "Danbury's burning! Gather at Ludington's!" She stopped only to hide when she spotted any British soldiers. She knew they would have captured her as a traitor!

(3) The next morning, the mud-splashed girl returned home. And 400 Minutemen marched against the British. When George Washington heard of Sybil's ride, he came to personally thank the brave young patriot.

11. Which is the main problem in the story?
 a. General Washington needed the Minutemen to find him a horse.
 b. Mr. Ludington needed to get a doctor to help Sybil.
 c. Someone had to rally the Minutemen to meet at Ludington's.
 d. Sybil needed to find a date for the spring dance.

12. What was the solution to the main problem?
   a. Sybil asked her older brother to take a message to their dad.
   b. Sybil rode to tell the Minutemen to gather at her house.
   c. Mr. Ludington sent a text message to each of the Minutemen.
   d. General Washington gave a speech to rally the troops.

13. How did Sybil solve the problem if she ran into any British soldiers?
   a. She fought them off with a sword.
   b. She fed them poisoned apples.
   c. Her horse knocked them down.
   d. She hid by the side of the road.

ANSWERS

1. d
2. a
3. b
4. d
5. b
6. d
7. a
8. b
9. a
10. Three of the following: lift heavy things, weld, spray paint, pack products, mix chemicals
11. c
12. b
13. d

making inferences

It is not really difficult to construct a series of inferences, each dependent upon its predecessor and each simple in itself.

SIR ARTHUR CONAN DOYLE (1859–1930)
BRITISH AUTHOR, "SHERLOCK HOLMES"

In this lesson, you'll discover you can use what you already know, plus clues from the text, to figure out things an author doesn't tell you outright!

SOMETIMES AN AUTHOR doesn't tell you exactly what's happening, but gives you clues so you can figure it out yourself.

An **inference** is a logical guess you make based on facts in the text *plus* what you already know from life. Maybe you or a friend have had a similar experience. Or maybe you read about something similar in a book or saw it in a movie. You can put the facts and personal knowledge together to figure out what's going on and why characters act or feel the way they do.

Example

A soaked Randy slipped inside the door and put his dripping umbrella in the corner. As he crossed the room to our table, his shoes made a squishy, squeaking sound. "What a day!" he moaned as he plopped into a chair and grabbed a menu.

The author didn't state what the weather was like or where the people were, but you can infer the answers. Clues in the text and your own experiences help you infer that a soaked Randy and dripping umbrella indicate it's raining outside. Randy going to a table and getting a menu helps you infer he's in a restaurant! Some people call making an inference "reading between the lines."

Making inferences helps good readers better understand the text. Inferring also builds readers' interest as they continue reading to find out if their inferences were or weren't correct.

An inference chart can help you track guesses as you read. List details you find in the text, what you already know, and what you infer from them.

The text says . . .	I know . . .	So I infer that . . .
Randy is wet. shoes squish and squeak. he has umbrella.	you use umbrellas in rain. you get soaked in rainstorms.	it's raining hard.
he comes inside. he goes to "our" table. he grabs a menu.	restaurants have menus. restaurants have tables. people share tables in restaurants.	he's in a restaurant.

PRACTICE 1: NOTICING NUMBERS

Read the selection, and then answer the questions that follow.

(1) My math teacher, Mr. Reyman, always comes up with really great ideas. Take for example our assignment last weekend. We thought he'd ask us to study for the upcoming test. Instead, on Friday he says, "Some of you have questioned our need to study fractions and how often people really use them in everyday life. So to answer your query, I want you to go on a fraction hunt this weekend!"

(2) Raquelita raises her hand and asks, "You mean bring in like part of a fraction, like one shoe because it's half of a whole pair?"

(3) "Or bring me," Paco laughs, "since I play baseball, I'm $\frac{1}{9}$ of a team?"

(4) "You've got it," Mr. Reyman agrees. "Actually bring things or just draw them. Your families can help. Let's see who can find the most interesting!"

(5) At dinner that night, I tell Dad and Mom about the assignment. "Sounds like fun," Mom says. "I bought new shoes today. They're size $6\frac{1}{2}$."

(6) "Great! I'm on my way!" I say as I draw a shoe with a $6\frac{1}{2}$ label inside.

(7) In the kitchen, I spot measuring cups with $\frac{1}{4}$, $\frac{1}{2}$, and $\frac{2}{3}$ on them and a measuring spoon labeled $\frac{1}{3}$. Dad brings in his toolbox and says, "Look in here. You'll find lots of fractions!" I do, wrenches labeled $\frac{1}{4}$, $\frac{5}{16}$, $\frac{3}{8}$, $\frac{7}{16}$, $\frac{9}{16}$, $\frac{5}{8}$, $\frac{11}{16}$, $\frac{3}{4}$, $\frac{13}{16}$, and $\frac{7}{8}$!

(8) Over the next two days, we find many other things. Dad asks, "Did you know hats come in fractional sizes?"

(9) "No, I usually see them labeled small, medium, and large!" I reply.

(10) Dad laughs and shows me his hat with a tag inside labeled $6\frac{7}{8}$. "I used to wear a $7\frac{3}{8}$," he chuckles. "My head must be getting smaller . . . or maybe I just had more hair then!"

(11) In the Sunday paper, I notice ads for sales, where things are $\frac{1}{2}$ or $\frac{1}{3}$ off. And Sunday night Dad shows me something special he has with a fraction written on it. "You can take this to school, but just be very careful with it," he says as he wraps it carefully in a soft cloth and puts it into a bag. "It's one of my favorites . . . and kind of rare."

(12) Monday everyone brings bags of stuff and lots of pictures to class. Other kids have wrenches, measuring utensils, and clothes. But no one else has the special thing my Dad gave me. "Wow!" says Mr. Reyman when I take it carefully out of the bag. "An old Beatles record!"

(13) He holds the record up for everyone to see. There, on the label, is the fraction and some letters: $33\frac{1}{3}$ RPM. Mr. Reyman explains that the letters stand for *Revolutions Per Minute* . . . the number of times the record spins around on a turntable each minute. He adds that today, CDs spin at between 200 and 500 RPM and produce a cleaner, clearer sound.

(14) We all agree that fractions are useful and people do use them a lot in everyday life. I wonder what fun assignment Mr. Reyman will think up next?

1. What can you infer from the first paragraph?
   a. Mr. Reyman is a new teacher in the school.
   b. The kids need to practice for the school musical.
   c. There's an important math test coming up soon.
   d. Most of the kids don't understand meteorology.

2. Why might you infer that the narrator's father is bald?
   a. He likes to wear hats.
   b. He said he used to have more hair.
   c. The narrator said he had a shiny head.
   d. The hat fit the narrator.

3. What can you infer about the fraction find?
   a. Some kids couldn't find anything with a fraction on it.
   b. Raquelita found the most interesting item.
   c. Paco brought in his whole team.
   d. The Beatles record was the most interesting thing.

4. From the story, what can you infer about the narrator's family?
   a. They get along well together.
   b. They argue a lot.
   c. They live in a trailer.
   d. They don't have time to do things together.

PRACTICE 2: ANCIENT ANIMALS

Read the selection, and then answer the questions that follow.

(1)   Dinosaurs are everywhere. You see them in movies, books, museums, and TV documentaries. They show up as stuffed toys or on T-shirts. These prehistoric beasts may be extinct—no longer living—but they're definitely not forgotten!

(2)   It's been a long time since dinosaurs roamed and ruled Earth. Scientists say the last ones died about 65 million years ago. We know the dinosaurs are gone, but no one knows exactly why. After all, no one was here to witness what happened! Most scientists believe dinosaurs died out after a gigantic meteorite hit Earth's surface and drastically changed the planet's climate. Birds and mammals that were protected by feathers and fur, were better able to adapt to the weather changes than cold-blooded dinosaurs.

(3)   Other scientists say dinosaurs aren't extinct, they just look different! These experts believe the prehistoric beasts changed and developed into birds! Still other scientists say that Earth's warmer weather caused more male than female dinosaurs to develop. So, they say, dinosaurs died out because there were no more females to increase the population!

(4)   How do scientists know what dinosaurs looked like? There were no cameras millions of years ago, so dinosaurs are the only ones who know . . . and they're not talking! Scientists get clues from dinosaur fossils, and infer the rest.

(5)   Bones, footprints, and other remains are evidence of how big dinosaurs were and how they moved. To figure out how they looked with their skin on, scientists look at animals that live today. Because dinosaurs were lizard-like, scientists can infer that dinosaurs looked a lot like modern-day lizards. And since modern lizards are brown, gray, or green, then dinosaurs probably were, too! That's why dinosaur pictures and museum models have the same colors as today's lizard populations.

(6)   Scientists are always discovering new things about dinosaurs. In recent years, fossils were found in Antarctica, proving that dinosaurs lived on every continent. Experts also figured out that Stegosaurus had only one spread-out row of plates down its back, not two individual rows. And fossils of the smallest and the largest dinosaurs have been found. What will scientists discover next?

5. From the first paragraph, you can infer that
   a. you can see dinosaurs only in museums.
   b. all dinosaurs were very tall.
   c. the author doesn't like dinosaurs.
   d. people of all ages are interested in dinosaurs.

6. Scientists found a rare blue lizard in Colombia, so you can infer that
   a. the scientists were looking for missing people.
   b. some dinosaurs might have been blue.
   c. no dinosaurs had ever lived in Colombia.
   d. the lizards built nests near the top of a volcano.

7. Since scientists are always discovering new things about dinosaurs, you can infer that
   a. they still might not have found the smallest or biggest dinosaurs.
   b. science is no longer interested in looking for fossils.
   c. prehistoric people left written records with descriptions of dinosaurs.
   d. when scientists make inferences, they are always right.

8. What can you infer from the fact that Stegosaurus has just one row of plates?
   a. Stegosaurus wasn't as old as scientists thought.
   b. Old pictures and museum models of Stegosaurus had to be changed.
   c. Someone stole the other row of plates from a museum.
   d. Stegosaurus means "roof lizard."

9. What can you infer about lizard eggs?
   a. Cooler temperatures should produce more female lizards.
   b. Hot weather should produce female lizards.
   c. Cold temperatures will produce more male lizards.
   d. Hot weather will produce more orange lizards.

10. What can you infer about scientists?
    a. They never watch TV.
    b. All scientists study about dinosaurs.
    c. They don't always agree.
    d. They never make mistakes.

PRACTICE 3: TOADSTOOL OR MUSHROOM?

Read the selection, and then answer the questions that follow.

(1) All toadstools are mushrooms, but not all mushrooms are toadstools!
     That's because toadstools are mushrooms that are either poisonous or
     have a bad taste. There are more than 2,000 mushroom species, and there's
     no simple test to tell the poisonous ones from those safe to eat! You just
     have to learn to recognize which is which.

(2) Most toadstools aren't deadly if eaten, but they're likely to make you very
     sick. For example, the Jack-o'-Lantern toadstool, whose bright orange cap
     glows in the dark, might give you an upset stomach or diarrhea. But some
     toadstools have deadly poison, and no amount of cooking can get rid of it.
     They damage the liver and kidneys, and unless the eater gets immediate
     treatment, he or she will die. That's why experts warn, *never* eat a mush-
     room you find growing anywhere unless you know it's the safe kind.

(3) Some of the loveliest toadstools are deadly. For example, the *fly agaric* has
     a bright yellow, orange, or red cap with white bumps on top. Some peo-
     ple cut up this deadly beauty, sprinkle it with sugar, and tempt pesky flies
     to drop in for a meal. If they do, they get the specialty of the house: instant
     death!

11. Which can you infer about mushrooms?
    a. They are all poisonous.
    b. They grow on soil.
    c. They are all yellow.
    d. They are all toadstools.

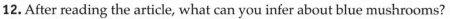

12. After reading the article, what can you infer about blue mushrooms?

    a. They are extremely poisonous.

    b. They are always safe to eat.

    c. They will upset your stomach.

    d. I don't have enough information to infer anything.

13. Which can you infer about mushrooms?

    a. They are very expensive.

    b. They are all flat.

    c. People cook them.

    d. They only grow under the ocean.

ANSWERS

    1. c

    2. b

    3. d

    4. a

    5. d

    6. b

    7. a

    8. b

    9. a

   10. c

   11. b

   12. d

   13. c

drawing conclusions

*People do not like to think. If one thinks, one must reach
conclusions. Conclusions are not always pleasant.*

HELEN KELLER (1880–1968)
AMERICAN AUTHOR AND LECTURER

In this lesson, you'll discover that you use clues from the text, plus any inferences you've made, to draw a conclusion about what's true and what isn't.

AFTER YOU MAKE one or more inferences, you can draw a **conclusion**—a decision based on facts and inferences. Drawing a conclusion is kind of like solving a mystery. You put together clues, or facts, from the text and all the inferences you made as you read it. Then you decide what's true. But be careful: Sometimes readers "jump to conclusions," or make decisions, before they have all the facts.

Example
Bo heard a classmate say she's going to Rome on summer vacation. He knows there's a famous city named Rome in Italy. So Bo sighs and says to a friend, "Dad says the price of gas is so high that we can't go away this summer. I wish I were going someplace really interesting . . . like Italy!"

Did Bo have enough information to draw that conclusion? No, he could infer that she meant Italy, but his inference was wrong. He jumped to that conclusion before he had all the facts. Imagine his surprise when he later finds out the girl always spends summers in Rome, Ohio!

Now, imagine you're the person in this story. What inferences can you make? What conclusion can you draw when you have all the facts?

Example

I couldn't believe it! I was set to go home and reached for my new jacket. But it was gone! I hunted for it everywhere around my locker. Suddenly I saw this kid walking out of school wearing a jacket just like mine! "Hey!" I yelled, "Wait up!"

Could you infer that the other kid took your missing jacket? Yes, but you be wrong and would be jumping to a conclusion. You need to ask questions and maybe examine the jacket. You do, and discover it looks like yours, but it's not. But you can conclude that the other kid has really good fashion sense, like you!

PRACTICE 1: GOOD ENOUGH FOR GRANDMA?

Read the selection, and then answer the questions that follow.

(1) Mom was busy in the kitchen when my brother Marco and I got home from school Friday. "Did you remember your grandmother's coming today?" she asked.

(2) "Sure, Mom," we laughed. "Didn't you notice we cleaned our rooms?"

(3) Mom smiled. "Thanks. I know I shouldn't be nervous, but my mother hasn't been here in almost six years! As I was growing up, her house always looked perfect. So I want everything to be . . . well . . ."

(4) "Perfect," I said with a smile. "What else can we do to help before she gets here?"

(5) Mom looked around, "You two could set the table. Use the good china . . . and be very careful with the glasses. . . . Grandma gave those to your dad and me before you were born!"

(6) As Mom prepared a sumptuous meal, Marco and I set the table. We carefully put a plate, glass, and silverware at each place. I taught Marco how to line up the forks on the left side of each plate and the knives and spoons on the right. In the center of the table, we placed a set of tall white candles. Then we stepped back and looked at our work. It seemed something was missing. "What's missing?" I asked Marco.

(7) "Napkins?" he asked. "And I don't think Mom would want us to use paper ones!"

(8) We both laughed. Marco opened a drawer and took out the nice cloth napkins Mom saved for special occasions. The soft white squares were folded in the middle, and we placed one on each plate. "Do you think that looks good enough?" I mumbled.

(9) "No," Marco whispered. "Let's make them look fancier. Remember that restaurant we went to last year? Their napkins were folded to look like crowns! Now that was elegant!"

(10) I nodded and unfolded the cloth napkin in front of me. "Look," I said, pointing to the creases in the cloth, "these lines make triangle shapes. That gives me a great idea! Let's do origami . . . that'll make the napkins unique!"

(11) Marco looked confused, so I explained, "Origami's a kind of folding art. People usually use paper, but you can use cloth. You make boats, birds, or flowers just by folding. No glue, tape, or staples are needed!"

(12) Mom overheard us. "I know how to make an origami bird and flower," she said. She quickly folded a napkin, then unfolded it to show us how the shapes fit together.

(13) Just then, Dad came home from work and showed us how to make a crown and a boat. "Okay," he said, "in 20 minutes your Grandma will walk through that door. Better get these napkins folded once and for all!"

(14) We did. We placed a different origami napkin on each plate. Now, the table looked elegant! And just in time.

(15) Grandma arrived by taxi and shared hugs all around. She gave us gifts from a bag labeled ORLY AIRPORT – PARIS. Then, as we walked into the dining room, she said, "Oh, my, who fixed these fabulous folded napkins? I've never seen anything so perfect!"

(16) We all smiled . . . happy that Grandma thought Mom's home was perfect, too!

  1. You can draw a conclusion that Marco is younger than the narrator because
    a. he wants to make the napkins look elegant.
    b. the narrator and he come home from school together.
    c. the narrator teaches him how to set a table and explains what origami is.
    d. he opens the drawer to get out the napkins.

2. Why might you conclude that Grandma lives in France?
   a. She came in a taxi.
   b. She had a bag labeled PARIS.
   c. She had not visited in six years.
   d. She liked to hug people.

3. What conclusion can you draw about an everyday meal at Marco's house?
   a. His dad never cooks.
   b. The family never has time to eat together.
   c. His mother is not a very good cook.
   d. The family uses paper napkins.

4. From the story, what can you conclude about the narrator and Marco?
   a. They usually don't keep their rooms clean!
   b. They very seldom go to bed on time!
   c. Spaghetti is their favorite food.
   d. They were named after their father's grandparents.

PRACTICE 2: TIME AFTER TIME

Read the selection, and then answer the questions that follow.

(1)   How do we know what time it is? Earth is divided into 24 time zones, one for each hour in a day. All locations within one zone share the same time.

Marking Meridians

(2)   How do we know where one time zone starts and another ends? Picture the world as a large orange—not that color or fruitiness, just that shape. Well, time zones are divided by *meridians*—imaginary lines that run from the North Pole to the South Pole (the top of the orange to the bottom). The meridians split the world into sections, like equal slices of orange. The prime, or zero, meridian runs through Greenwich, England. By international agreement in 1884, that's been the starting point from which all time is calculated.

Time Marches On

(3)   Doesn't it appear that the sun moves from east to west? Well, it doesn't. Earth actually turns from west to east as it rotates on its axis. And like Earth, time moves from west to east. So from that prime meridian in Greenwich, you add one hour for each time zone as you move east. You subtract one hour for each zone as you move west.

(4)   Let's say you're in London, England, and it's 3 P.M. on Monday. You want to know what time it is in Paris, France, to the east. Just add one hour for each time zone between the two cities and you'll discover it's 4 P.M. on Monday in Paris.

(5)   If you want to know the time to the west, subtract an hour per zone. You discover that when it's 3 P.M. on Monday in London, it's 10 A.M. in New York, 9 A.M. in Chicago, 8 A.M. in Denver, and 7 A.M. in Los Angeles. Farther west, across the Pacific Ocean, time continues to change hour by hour. Finally, about halfway around the world from England, an imaginary zigzag line forms the International Dateline . . . and suddenly it's another day! If it weren't, you'd continue going west and get back to London before you left! But instead, if it's 3 P.M. on Monday in London, it's 7 P.M. on *Tuesday* in Hong Kong!

5. If you lived in Chicago, what could you conclude about time in Denver?
   a. It would be one hour later than in Chicago.
   b. It would be the same time as in Chicago.
   c. It would be one hour earlier than in Chicago.
   d. It would be one day earlier than in Chicago.

6. If it were noon in Chicago, what could you conclude?
   a. It's one hour earlier in Denver.
   b. It's one hour later in New York.
   c. It's already the next day somewhere in the world.
   d. all of the above

7. You can conclude the time difference between Paris and Chicago is
   a. 6 hours.
   b. 7 hours.
   c. 8 hours.
   d. 9 hours.

8. What can you conclude from the words, *By international agreement . . .* in paragraph 2?
   a. Some countries don't have any time zones.
   b. Only the most important countries have time zones.
   c. All the countries of the world use these time zones.
   d. Some people in the world live in two time zones.

9. After reading the article, the best conclusion I can draw is that
   a. if you know the time in one place, you can figure out the time in other places.
   b. it's impossible to know what time it is halfway around the world.
   c. you should use only shadows from the sun to figure out the exact time.
   d. it should always be the same time everywhere!

PRACTICE 3: YOUR CROWNING GLORY

Read the selection, then answer the questions that follow.

(1) Human hair may be curly or straight, and either a blonde-haired person, red, brown, black, white, or a mixture thereof. But everyone's hair is relatively the same in the way it grows.

(2) Hair is a threadlike structure that grows from the skin. Below the scalp, at the bottom of each hair, is a tiny pit called a *follicle*. It leads down to the hair's root. Cells at the base of the root begin to move up. As they do, they harden and become a strand of hair.

(3) The hair on your head grows in stages. Follicles actively produce hair for three to six years, then rest for about three months. There's an average of 100,000 hairs on the human head, and about 10% are resting at any given time. We lose about 70–100 hairs every day from our resting follicles!

(4) Sometimes it seems your hair grows fast, but it normally grows less than $\frac{1}{2}$ inch (13 mm) a month. Children's hair grows faster than adults' hair, and everyone's hair grows faster in summer than winter!

10. You can conclude that about 90% of the follicles on your head
   a. are resting and not producing hair.
   b. are too small to hold the root of a hair.
   c. are producing hair at this time.
   d. have been closed and can't produce a hair.

11. If it is winter, you can conclude that
  a. your hair is growing slower than it did last summer.
  b. your hair is growing faster than it did last summer.
  c. your hair is growing the same as it did last summer.
  d. you have fewer follicles than you had last summer.

12. What might you logically conclude about the growth of hair in summer?
  a. More people get their hair cut in hot summer weather.
  b. Cold weather makes plants and hair grow longer.
  c. Wearing a hat in winter stops hair growth.
  d. Heat and sweat make hair grow faster.

ANSWERS

  1. c
  2. b
  3. d
  4. a
  5. c
  6. d
  7. b
  8. c
  9. a
  10. c
  11. a
  12. d

summarizing

In three words I can sum up everything
I've learned about life: It goes on.
ROBERT FROST (1874–1963) AMERICAN POET

In this lesson, you'll discover that you can retell a story in just a few sentences and still hit the most important points!

A SUMMARY IS a short retelling of a story or an event. You summarize every time you tell friends about your vacation or a movie you saw. You can't tell everything, so you tell what's most important: the main idea and a few details. Usually, you can do this in just a few sentences. Here's an event and summary:

What Happened

Sara goes shopping at the mall over the weekend. She runs into an old friend, Chris, who'd moved away last year. They have lunch together and Sara discovers that Chris's family will be moving back to town next month, so he'll be going to her school again. Chris says he hopes he'll be able to get back on the school soccer team since he's on a winning team where he's been living.

Sara's Summary: Guess who I ran into at the mall, whose family's moving back to town? Chris . . . and he thinks he'll probably be back on our soccer team!

You can summarize a story or article; or just a part of it.

Text
Archaeologists learn about the past by studying things ancient people left behind. The people can be grouped by the technology they used: Stone Age people used stone tools; Bronze Age people first made metal tools. A painting or carving may show people in carts. That's technology. Scraps of material are clues to how people used technology to make clothing. And written journals tell how people used technology to make medicines from plants.

Summary: Scientists find evidence of how people used technology during their lifetimes. Different technologies were used at different times in history to make tools, clothing, art, vehicles, and medicines.

Posters, book covers, and ads are summaries. They give all the most important information about something in a small space! Sometimes you have to write or give an oral book report, and on many tests, you're asked to write a short essay about a selection. That's why it's important to learn to look for the most important facts and sharpen your summarizing skills!

PRACTICE 1: *THE GIFT OF THE MAGI*

Based on a story by O. Henry

Read the selection; then answer the questions that follow.

(1) One dollar and eighty-seven cents. That was all she had. And the next day would be Christmas. Della flopped down on the shabby old couch and cried. She wanted so much to get something special for her husband Jim, but she only had $1.87. Della stood and looked at herself in the mirror. Her eyes were red. She didn't want Jim to know she'd been crying. She let her hair fall to its full length, almost to her knees, and began to brush it. Jim loved her soft, long hair. The only thing he liked more was the gold watch that had belonged to his father and grandfather.

(2) Suddenly Della had an idea. She piled her hair on top of her head, put on her old brown jacket and hat, and fluttered out the door and down the steps to the street. She stopped at a door that read: *Madame Sofron, Hair Goods.* Della ran in and asked, "Will you buy my hair?"

(3) "Take off your hat and let me see," said Madame Sofron. She looked at Della's shiny hair and said, "I can give you 20 dollars."

(4) For two hours, Della went from store to store, looking for a special gift for Jim. At last, she found it . . . a simple gold watch chain. It would replace the old leather strap he now used on his beloved watch!

(5) When Della got home, she fixed her head in short close-lying curls. She looked in the mirror, satisfied with the new look. She had dinner ready by 7 o'clock, but Jim had not come home. Della began to worry; he was never late. At last she heard him come up the steps. The door opened and in walked Jim. "You've cut off your hair!" he said sadly when he saw Della.

(6) "I sold it," said Della. "But I'm still me, aren't I?"

(7) "Of course," Jim said softly as he took a package from his coat pocket. "But if you'll unwrap this package you'll see why I am sad."

(8) Della's fingers tore at the string and paper. Inside she found a set of combs she'd once admired in a shop window. They were beautiful, with jeweled rims that would have looked magnificent in her handsome, long hair.

(9) "Oh, Jim, how lovely," she cried. "I shall wear them when my hair grows. It grows fast. But see," she added happily, "I have a gift for you!"

(10) Della held out the watch chain in her open palm. "I hunted all over town to find it. Give me your watch. I want to see how it looks on it!"

(11) Instead, Jim sat on the couch and began to laugh. "Oh, Della," he said, "I sold my watch to get the money to buy your combs!"

(12) Della sat beside him and together they laughed. They were happy, yet sad, to know that each had given up a prized possession for the love of the other. It was a special Christmas that year, a day filled with love.

1. A summary is a retelling of a story that
   a. is always shorter than the original text.
   b. must be at least two paragraphs long.
   c. has no ending.
   d. gives new information that was not in the story.

2. Which is the best one-sentence summary for paragraph 1?
   a. Della is sad because Jim sold his watch.
   b. Della is sad because she doesn't have much money to buy a gift for Jim.
   c. Della is sad because her mother can't come to visit.
   d. Della is sad because she has no new coat to wear.

3. Which would NOT be important to include in a summary of the story?

    a. Della has beautiful long hair.

    b. Jim has a gold watch that belonged to his father and grandfather.

    c. Della wanted something special for Jim.

    d. Della and Jim lived in an apartment.

4. Which is the main idea of the story?

    a. Della changes her hairstyle.

    b. Jim and Della plan a special Christmas dinner.

    c. Jim and Della sacrifice to get each other special gifts.

    d. Della only has old clothing to wear.

5. Write a summary of the story. Try to summarize in just a few sentences.

_____

_____

_____

_____

PRACTICE 2: WATER, WATER EVERYWHERE!

Read the selection; then answer the questions that follow.

(1) Is a flood ever good news? How can it be? When river water overflows and floods the land, people can lose their homes . . . even their lives! So to people who live in flood-prone areas, a flood is always bad news. But in ancient Egypt, things were different. The people looked forward to a yearly flood and saw it as good news!

(2) Many Egyptians lived and farmed by the Nile River, which flooded every summer. They eagerly anticipated the event because they knew that when the water receded, the land would be better for crops. That's because floodwaters carry along washed-away soil and sediment, then drop it somewhere else. There, the nutrients in the sediment sink into and nourish the land. Then the farmland is richer and ready for crops.

(3) The Egyptians weren't sure why the flood came each year. Many believed it was a gift from the spirits, who sent great clouds of rain to fall near the source of the Nile. But actually, that wasn't the case. The annual flood was caused by natural events that began high in the mountains of Ethiopia.

(4)   In June, strong winds from the South Atlantic Ocean blow over the rainforests of Africa. When the winds reach Ethiopia's mountains, some of which are 13,000 feet (4,000 m) high, giant rain clouds drop their contents in huge thunderstorms. The rain continues and mountain streams fill to the brim. Then the streams join together to form a sizeable river. It speeds along to meet the Nile, carrying lots of soil and sediment with it. By July, the rushing water reaches Egypt, where it produces a flood in the Nile.

(5)   The yearly flooding of the Nile wasn't all good news. Sometimes buildings and fences were swept away and property lines disappeared. But landowners just marked off their territories and put up new fences for another year.

(6)   Today, floodwaters from Ethiopia are stopped soon after they reach Egypt. A large dam on the river holds back the rushing, rising water and forms a large lake. This is good news. Now buildings and fences aren't swept away. And today farmers can plant two crops a year instead of just one.

(7)   But the dam is bad news, too. The waters of the yearly flood always kept the fields fertile. Today, farmers use fertilizers that get into the mud and water of the Nile. Fish that once thrived in the Nile are gone. And a serious disease is spread by snails that live in the slow-moving waters of the great river.

(8)   So back to our original question: Is a flood ever good news? As you can see, it can be, if the good benefits outweigh the bad.

  6. Which is the best one-sentence summary for paragraph 2?
    a. A yearly flood in Egypt did a lot of damage.
    b. A yearly flood in Egypt brought sediment that helped the land.
    c. A yearly flood brought more people to Ethiopia.
    d. A yearly flood in Egypt was caused by rain over the Pacific Ocean.

  7. Which is the best summary for paragraph 4?
    a. Winds from the Atlantic drop rain on Egypt at the source of the Nile. The rain floods large cities near the river.
    b. Rain over the Atlantic comes on shore in Egypt and floods the Nile.
    c. Rain in France forms a river that travels to Egypt and dumps into the Nile. Then the Nile floods Egyptian farmland beside the river.
    d. Winds from the Atlantic drop rain on Ethiopia and rain-filled streams form a river. It dumps into the Nile, which floods Egyptian farmland beside the river.

8. Which would be an important detail to include in a summary of the article?
   a. The Nile River is in Egypt.
   b. People sail boats on the Nile.
   c. The capital of Ethiopia is Addis-Ababa.
   d. The Mississippi River also floods sometimes.

9. Write a summary of the whole article. Try to summarize in just two or three sentences.

   _____

   _____

   _____

   _____

PRACTICE 3: FOODS AROUND THE WORLD

Read the selection, and then answer the questions that follow.

(1)   Why do people in different places eat different foods? One reason is that humans store energy as starch or fat. People eat local plants that provide starch and fat, but not all plants grow everywhere!

(2)   **Europe and the Middle East**   For thousands of years, people have used wheat, a wild grass, as their main starch. In the Mediterranean, people use olive oil to provide fat. In the north, few plants produce oils, so people use animal fat.

(3)   **Asia**   Rice, a wild grass, is the main starch of Southeast Asia. In northern Asia, it's too cold to grow rice, so people use wheat. The Chinese cook with soybean or peanut oils. In India, people use butter or sesame seed oil.

(4)   **The Americas**   Potatoes are the main starch in Peru and other places. Corn, or maize, was once the main starch in North America. It still is in Mexico.

(5)   **The Tropics**   Wheat, rice, corn, and potatoes are hard to grow in the tropics. So many people use a starchy tuber called a yucca, manioc, or cassava. Palm and coconut oil are also popular forms of fat in tropical regions.

10. Which is the best one-sentence summary of the section about Europe?

   a. Most people eat yucca and get fats from corn oil.

   b. Most people use rice to make bread and get fats from olives.

   c. Most people use wheat to make bread and get fats from olive oil.

   d. Most people use corn to make bread and get fats from yucca oil.

11. Which is the best summary of the whole article?

   a. Local plants supply starch and fat for humans. So people in different regions eat different foods, depending on what grows in their area.

   b. Corn grows only in some places. People who can't get corn eat olives to get starch.

   c. Local plants supply sugars for humans. So, people in all regions eat sweet food that can be grown all over the world.

   d. Rice grows almost anywhere. People who can't get rice can get fats from wheat.

ANSWERS

   1. a

   2. b

   3. d

   4. c

   5. Sample summary: Della sells her beautiful long hair to buy a chain for her husband Jim's gold watch and he sells the watch to buy combs for her hair. Each gives up something special for the one they love.

   6. b

   7. d

   8. a

   9. Sample summary: Floods on the Nile in ancient Egypt made farmland fertile with sediment carried by the water. Today a dam stops the flooding, but modern fertilizers pollute the river and the water is home to disease-carrying snails.

   10. c

   11. a

SECTION 4

elements of literature: the facts about fiction

LITERARY ELEMENTS ARE some special things authors use to make their fiction stories more interesting. Authors often choose words that may not mean exactly what they say, or words that suggest a feeling rather than just state a fact. And authors may use special words to help readers visualize people, places, and events of a story. In this section of the book, you'll discover how to

- analyze characters and settings.
- recognize the conflicts and solutions of a plot.
- identify the point of view.
- recognize the theme of a story.
- understand the use of imagery.
- analyze the use of flashback and foreshadowing.
- recognize the use of idioms, personification, and hyperbole.
- discern the difference between similes and metaphors.

character and setting

We can't all be heroes because somebody has to sit
on the curb and clap as they go by.
WILL ROGERS (1879–1935)
CHEROKEE-AMERICAN COWBOY, HUMORIST, AND ACTOR

In this lesson, you'll discover who's in a story, and when and where the events take place are very important.

CHARACTERS ARE THE people, animals, or lifelike objects in a story. Since the author makes up the characters, they can be anything he or she wishes, from real-life humans to aliens to talking cars! Characters show what they're like through their words and actions, and how they respond to other characters.

Example
In Persia, there lived two brothers: Casmir and Ali Baba. Brothers they were, but as different as day and night. Casmir, the older brother, married a rich woman, though she was often mean to him and others. He became a wealthy merchant. But Ali Baba married a sweet girl who was very, very poor. Love he had, but he had to work hard cutting wood and selling it in the marketplace.

Each character, like those in *Ali Baba and the 40 Thieves* and other stories in this book, has special traits, or qualities. One character may be tall, angry, and dishonest. Another may be gentle, thoughtful, and heroic. Having a variety of characters in a story makes it more interesting.

The setting of a story is where and when it takes place. In *Ali Baba*, it was Persia. Most stories have more than one setting. Each is important to what happens in the story.

Example
On Saturday morning, the family packed the car and left for a camping trip on Mount Vista. Later that day, Mr. Maxim and the two boys left their campsite and headed up the mountain. A sudden snowstorm swept through the area that night. And Monday morning a distressed Mrs. Maxim walked to the nearest state police post to report that her husband and boys were missing.

Here the settings are the family home, the campsite, and the police station. As you read, note different characters and settings, and how a setting can influence what characters do or how they speak. For example, at home Mrs. Maxim might be very calm and friendly, but at the police station, she may stammer or cry as she speaks very formally to the officers.

PRACTICE 1: *THE FOX AND THE CROW*

An Aesop's Fable Retold

Read the selection, and then answer the questions that follow.

(1)   Crow landed high in a tree, holding in her beak a bit of meat she'd found nearby. Below the tree walked Fox, who looked up when he heard a flutter of leaves. He saw Crow and the meat dangling from her beak.

(2)   Fox wanted the meat, so he deceitfully said to no one at all, "How handsome is that Crow! So beautiful and shiny are her feathers! Ah, if only her voice were equal to her beauty, she would be considered the Queen of Birds!"

(3)   Now Crow, being very vain, heard Fox's flattery of her appearance and was pleased. But she was also anxious to prove him wrong about her voice. So she opened her beak and let out a loud CAW, CAW, dropping the meat as she did. Fox quickly picked it up and ate it. Then he looked up and laughed, "My good Crow, your voice is alright . . . it's your brain that's lacking!" And with that, he walked away, leaving the hungry Crow to feel sorry for herself.

1. What is the setting of the story?
   a. a fox's den
   b. a birdhouse
   c. a tree
   d. a boat on the river

2. Fox gets the meat from Crow because one of his character traits is being
   a. helpful.
   b. dishonest.
   c. sad.
   d. a good cook.

3. Which is NOT one of Crow's character traits?
   a. having feathers
   b. being vain
   c. having a loud voice
   d. being smart

PRACTICE 2: AN OPEN DOOR

Read the selection, and then answer the questions that follow.

(1)   "Oh, well," I sighed as I plopped down at the kitchen table. "There goes a great chapter in my life!"

(2)   Mom looked up from the batter she was mixing. "What's the matter? Why are you so down in the dumps?" she asked.

(3)   "That was Mrs. Barberi on the phone. I didn't make the debate team this year!" I grumbled. "I don't know why I didn't do better!"

(4)   "Come on, Sam, don't be so hard on yourself!" Mom replied. "You know there are money problems everywhere. The school had to limit funds for some programs and the debate team was cut in half this year."

(5)   "I know . . . ," I sighed. "But I still wanted to make it. I like debating, and getting to go to other schools around the state to compete is a lot of fun! I met a lot of new kids that way!"

(6)   Mom smiled. "I know you did, but like people say, *When life shuts a door in your face, another door opens*"!

(7)   "I think it's a window, Mom," I said. "*If a door closes a window opens.*"

(8) "Whatever," Mom laughed. "The point is that something else will come
along . . . maybe even better, 'cause you don't know what lies beyond that
door . . . I mean, window!"

(9) We were interrupted by the sound of the phone ringing in the living room.
"I'll get it," I said. "It's probably Chris wanting to tell me about all the fun
stuff the rest of the debate team will do without me this year!"

(10) I picked up the phone, expecting to hear Chris's voice. But it was someone else. I listened attentively, thanked the caller, and went into the
kitchen again.

(11) "You look funny . . . who was it . . . is something wrong?" asked Mom, and
she jumped up from the table.

(12) "Not wrong, just strange!" I replied. "That was Mr. Diaz, from school."

(13) "So? What did he want?" Mom asked anxiously.

(14) "Me," I replied with a smile. "He wants me to take the lead in the school
play! He said I was awesome at the auditions! I'd almost forgotten I tried
out this year . . . it was way before the holidays! Mom . . . I got the lead!"

(15) "You see, Sam," Mom said as she grabbed me and we whirled in a circle.
"Another door opened and you'll start a whole new chapter of your life!"

(16) "Window, Mom," I sighed, "window!"

4. The main setting for this story is
    a. a school.
    b. a hallway.
    c. a living room.
    d. a kitchen.

5. What is the other setting of the story?
    a. a school
    b. a hallway
    c. a living room
    d. an auditorium

6. Which best describes Sam at the beginning of the story?
    a. excited about getting on the debate team
    b. depressed about not getting a part in the play
    c. excited about trying out for the play
    d. depressed about not getting on the debate team

7. Which is NOT a character trait of Sam's mother?

    a. concerned

    b. annoyed

    c. sympathetic

    d. encouraging

8. Which best describes a trait both characters have?

    a. sense of humor

    b. distrust

    c. disgust

    d. jealousy

PRACTICE 3: *A STUDY IN SCARLET*

Excerpted and adapted from the story by A. Conan Doyle

Read the selection, and then answer the questions that follow.

(1)   It was 1878 and I had neither kith nor kin in England, much less money. I stayed for some time in a London hotel, but needed to move to less expensive housing. One day, I ran into Stamford, a friend from the army. "Dr. Watson," he said, "What have you been up to?"

(2)   "Looking for lodgings," I answered.

(3)   "That's strange," he remarked. "A fellow I know is looking for someone to go halves with him in some nice rooms which were too expensive for him."

(4)   "By Jove!" I cried. " I am the very man for him!"

(5)   Stamford looked rather strangely at me. "You don't know Sherlock Holmes yet," he said. "Perhaps you would not care for him as a constant companion."

(6)   "Why, what is there against him?" I asked.

(7)   "Oh, I didn't say there was anything against him. As far as I know he is a decent fellow enough, just a little . . . odd."

(8)   Stamford took me to the hospital where he worked to meet this Sherlock Holmes. "Dr. Watson, Mr. Sherlock Holmes," said Stamford, introducing us.

(9) "How are you?" Holmes said cordially, gripping my hand with strength. "You have been in Afghanistan, I observe."

(10) "How on earth did you know that?" I asked in astonishment.

(11) "Never mind," said he, chuckling to himself.

(12) Holmes seemed delighted at the idea of sharing rooms. "I have my eye on a place in Baker Street," he said. "Occasionally I do experiments. Would that annoy you?"

(13) "By no means," I said. "I get up at all sorts of hours, and am extremely lazy."

(14) "Oh, that's all right!" he cried, with a merry laugh. "I think we may consider the thing as settled—that is, if the rooms are agreeable to you."

(15) They were, so we moved into 221B, Baker Street. As we settled in, Holmes said, "You were surprised when I said, on our first meeting, that you had come from Afghanistan."

(16) "You were told, no doubt," I declared.

(17) "Nothing of the sort," he replied. "I arrived at the conclusion through observation. You are a doctor, and I concluded by the tan of your skin that you were just back from the eastern part of the world. Your face showed that you had recently been sick, and your left arm was injured. I asked myself, 'Where in the east could an English army doctor have got his arm wounded?' Clearly in Afghanistan."

(18) "It is simple enough as you explain it," I said, smiling.

9. What is the main setting of this story?
   a. London, England, in 1978
   b. London, Ontario, in 1789
   c. London, England, in 1878
   d. London, England, in 1808

10. Who are the two main characters in the story?
   a. Dr. Watson and Stamford
   b. Dr. Watson and Sherlock Holmes
   c. Sherlock Holmes and Stamford
   d. none of the above

11. Which best describes the character of Sherlock Holmes?
    a. unreasonable
    b. gloomy
    c. observant
    d. dim-witted

12. Holmes proves he's a considerate person when he
    a. sees that Watson needs money and offers a loan.
    b. notices Watson's bad arm and offers him a cane.
    c. asks if Watson would like to have lunch.
    d. asks if doing experiments would annoy Watson.

13. In which setting does Holmes explain how he knew about Watson and Afghanistan?
    a. a hotel coffee shop
    b. a Baker Street apartment
    c. a London hospital
    d. an army depot

ANSWERS

1. c
2. b
3. d
4. d
5. c
6. d
7. b
8. a
9. c
10. b
11. c
12. d
13. b

● L ● E ● S ● S ● O ● N ● **24**

plot: conflict and resolution

A story to me means a plot where there is some surprise.
Because that is how life is—full of surprises.
ISAAC BASHEVIS SINGER (1904–1991)
POLISH-BORN AMERICAN WRITER

In this lesson, you'll discover how events flow in sequence to create a story about someone's problem and how it gets solved!

A PLOT IS the sequence of events in a story. The beginning, or **exposition**, explains a character's **conflict**, or problem. The main part tells how the character tries to solve the problem with *rising action* that leads to a **climax**, or turning point. That's when someone usually realizes how to solve the problem. Then there's *falling action* that leads to the **resolution**, or end. It tells how the problem is finally solved, or occasionally, it not solved. Some people might call that an unhappy ending!

Here's a look at plot parts, using the familiar story of the Pilgrims' 1620 voyage on the *Mayflower*.

THE PILGRIM STORY: BASIC PLOT

Exposition	tells the problem, or conflict	Some people in seventeenth-century England are persecuted. They need to go somewhere safe.
Rising Action	main part of the story	In September 1620, some 102 people, along with their animals, furniture, and supplies needed for a new life, head for America aboard *Mayflower* over rough seas. On the grueling 65-day voyage, many people are sick, some die, and a baby is born.
Climax	turning point toward a solution to the problem	November 9: The crew spots land off Cape Cod, Massachusetts. The ship heads south to Virginia, where Pilgrims have permission to settle. Bad weather and dangerously shallow water force the captain to turn back north.
Falling Action	events from the climax to the solution	November 11: The ship lands in Massachusetts. The Pilgrims come ashore to explore the area. They decide to settle in Plymouth, and live on the ship while building on shore.
Resolution	problem is solved	Early 1621: The Pilgrims move into their new homes in America at Plimouth Plantation.

Use a plot diagram like the one on the opposite page to follow the action as you read. The graphic organizer will help you recall important facts for summaries or test questions.

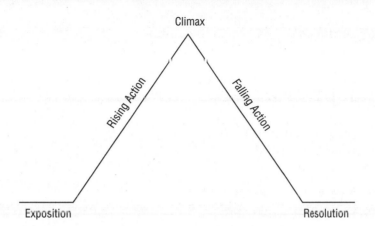

PRACTICE 1: NO EXIT

Read the selection, and then answer the questions that follow.

(1)   As the robot came closer, Zantur knew it would be almost impossible to escape. He slipped around a corner and held his breath as the metallic monitor clanked by. Zantur was determined to get out. . . . He didn't know why he'd let the others talk him into coming in the first place! They knew of his fear, yet they persisted, taunting him until he agreed to join them. But now . . . now he just couldn't go through with it! He carefully peered around the corner. The robot was nowhere in sight, so Zantur inched his way toward an EXIT sign flashing ahead of him. Just as he reached out to unlatch the pod covering, the robot grabbed his arm. "CAUGHT! CAUGHT!" it beeped loudly.

(2)   People came rushing down the hall. "Aha! It was you!" someone shouted. "Are you just getting here . . . trying to get in through a latched pod door?"

(3)   Zantur pulled his arm from the robot's clutch. "Ye-ye-yeah!" he stammered. "Sorry to be late. I'm really looking forward to this!" Then he forced a smile as he joined his graduating class in the dance room for the prom. He looked at Debu and she shyly smiled. He so wished he wasn't afraid to ask her to dance!

1. What is the main conflict in this story?
   a. Zantur doesn't want to go to the prom.
   b. Zantur needs to hide from the robot monitor.
   c. Zantur forgot to get Debu flowers for the dance.
   d. Debu wants Zantur to ask her to dance.

2. Zantur plans to solve his problem by
   a. taking dance lessons.
   b. dismantling the robot.
   c. escaping from the building.
   d. playing in the dance band.

3. How does Zantur resolve the problem?
   a. He opens the pod and escapes.
   b. He doesn't because he still has to go to the dance.
   c. He decides he likes to dance.
   d. He hides in a closet all night.

PRACTICE 2: *UNEQUAL WAGES*

Adapted from a Russian Folk Tale

Read the selection, and then answer the questions that follow.

(1) Mr. Moscov was a rich man who had many workers in his factory. He treated them all well and they were fond of him. They knew he was honest and would often ask for his advice.

(2) John and Joseph were two such workers. John was paid $4.00 a week, and Joseph was paid $10.00. John's job was very hard. He moved heavy furniture and carried hefty boxes up and down the stairs. But Joseph only worked in a nice office, writing letters for Moscov and keeping the business records. So John often wondered why Joseph earned so much more money. Finally, he decided to ask Mr. Moscov. "Sir, something puzzles me," John said. "Can you please explain?"

(3) John told Moscov what was bothering him. Moscov listened attentively, then said, "Yes, I'll explain the difference between your wages and Joseph's, but first, do something for me. Do you see that loaded wagon in the driveway? Ask the driver, please, what he has in his load."

(4) John quickly went and did as he was asked. When he returned, he told Moscov the wagon was loaded with wheat. "Where is the wheat going?" asked Moscov.

(5) Again, John went outside to talk to the driver of the wagon. "The wheat is to be delivered in the next town," he reported when he returned.

(6) "And from where is the wheat coming?" Moscov asked.

(7) Once more John rushed outside, spoke to the wagon driver, and returned with the answer. Then Moscov wanted to know how much grain was in the load. As soon as John learned that, Moscov sent him back to ask how much the wheat was worth per bushel! A very weary John shuffled out again to the wagon. Altogether, he made six trips to get answers to Moscov's questions!

(8) Then Moscov sent for Joseph, who was in another room. "Joseph, please run out to that driver and ask him what he has in his wagon. I want to know."

(9) Quickly, Joseph ran out and was back in less time than it took John to ask his first question. "The driver is from Sinyava and is delivering a load of wheat from Svod to Brod," said Joseph. "He's been on the road since early morning and expects to arrive in Brod before nightfall. He's carrying 120 bushels of wheat, worth 75 cents a bushel. But, he says. the wheat crop is large this year, so he expects the price to fall before long. Is that all, Sir?"

(10) "Yes, thank you, Joseph," said Moscov.

(11) When Joseph left the room, Moscov turned to John. "Now, John," he said, "do you understand why Joseph earns more money than you?"

(12) John nodded. "Yes, Sir," he sighed, "he has to think while he works!"

4. The conflict in this story is that
    a. Joseph wants more money.
    b. Moscov has no time to listen to his employees.
    c. John wants to know why he makes less money than Joseph.
    d. John wants the driver of the wagon to come talk to Mosov.

5. How does John plan to resolve the conflict?
    a. Threaten to quit his job.
    b. Go on strike.
    c. Offer to loan Joseph some money.
    d. Ask Mr. Moscov why he pays Joseph more.

6. Which is part of the rising action?
   a. Mr. Moscov repeatedly sends John out to question a driver.
   b. Joseph drives the wagon to Brod.
   c. Mr. Moscov offers to buy the wheat.
   d. John and Joseph exchange jobs.

7. The climax of the story is when
   a. Joseph offers to work for less money.
   b. Mr. Moscov sends Joseph to give a letter to the driver.
   c. John helps the driver unload the wagon.
   d. Joseph goes outside only once and gets all the answers.

8. The conflict is resolved when John realizes that
   a. Joseph can carry heavy things, too!
   b. Mr. Moscov doesn't know why he pays Joseph more.
   c. using your brain can be hard work, too!
   d. the driver doesn't own the wheat he's delivering.

PRACTICE 3: NO EXIT 2: A PLOT CHANGE

The beginning may start like "No Exit" on page 211, but then the plot twists and the story changes!
   Read the selection, and then answer the questions that follow.

(1)   As the footsteps came closer, Ryan knew it would be almost impossible to escape. He slipped around a corner and held his breath as footsteps hurried by. He was determined to get out and get help. . . . He didn't know why he'd let the others talk him into coming in the first place! They had persisted, taunting him until he had agreed to join them. Now . . . now he just wanted out!

(2)   Ryan cautiously peered around the corner. There was no one in sight, so he inched his way down the silent hallway. It was so dark he could hardly see where he was going. Then he saw a beam of light and ducked low, crouching behind a large box just as someone came by. "Did you find him?" a hoarse voice murmured from somewhere below.

(3)   "No . . . I think he may have got out!" replied a nearby raspy voice. "But he's so scared he won't talk!"

(4) Ryan hardly breathed as the footsteps came closer, then faded away and he heard a door close. He wondered where his friends were. Had they been lucky enough to get out? For a moment, he was angry. After all, it'd been their idea to come to this empty old house . . . the one people thought was haunted!

(5) As a kid, Ryan was always afraid of the place . . . especially after his older brother had said there were monsters inside. Now he was here . . . and his so-called friends were somewhere else! They just wanted some scary fun, they'd said. How could they have known the old house was a meeting spot for drug dealers? How could they have anticipated running into a drug deal in the making? But they had . . . and so they had scattered, with some tough types chasing them! Now Ryan didn't know if anyone got out safely or not. But he was determined he would!

(6) All was quiet, so Ryan crept from room to room, looking for a way out. Finally, he spotted an unboarded window that was broken. As silently and carefully as possible, he slipped out. It was a long way down to the ground, but somehow he made it. Ryan ran for his life! Once he felt safe, he called 911 on his cell phone.

(7) The police quietly arrived shortly after that. They busted up the drug deal, arrested the dealers, and found the other kids.

(8) Ryan was happy to see that his friends were safe. They'd hunkered down in the cellar and waited. "We knew you'd get help," said his friend Greg.

(9) "Yeah?" replied Ryan. "Next time we might not be so lucky!"

(10) The stern voice of a police officer added, "There better never **be** a next time!"

(11) The next week, a crew tore down the old building to make way for a new one. A sign at the site read HOME OF THE NEW COMMUNITY CENTER.

9. What is the conflict in this story?
   a. Ryan is afraid of monsters.
   b. Ryan and his friends need to have some fun.
   c. Ryan needs to escape and call for help.
   d. Ryan needs to borrow Greg's cell phone.

10. Which is NOT part of the rising action?
   a. Ryan hides from the person who's chasing him.
   b. Ryan creeps from room to room.
   c. Ryan spots a broken window.
   d. Ryan says he doesn't want to go to the old house.

11. The climax of the story is when
    a. Ryan gets safely out and calls 911.
    b. Ryan finds a window through which he can escape.
    c. The friends hunker down in the cellar.
    d. Ryan hides behind a big box in the hall.

12. Which is part of the falling action?
    a. Ryan sees a light in the hallway.
    b. Greg and the others walk in on a drug deal.
    c. Ryan runs for his life and calls 911.
    d. One of the dealers follows Ryan.

13. The conflict is resolved when
    a. the police come to help Ryan and his friends.
    b. a community center opens in town.
    c. the police warn the kids not to come back.
    d. the dealers leave in their car.

ANSWERS

  1. a
  2. c
  3. b
  4. c
  5. d
  6. a
  7. d
  8. c
  9. c
10. d
11. b
12. c
13. a

point of view

In this lesson, you'll find that it's important to know who's telling you a story because a narrator's point of view can change how you feel about things you read.

A NARRATOR IS a person who tells a story. The narrator may be one of the characters in the story, so readers learn what happened from that character's point of view. This is called the **first-person** point of view. The narrator uses words like *I*, *me*, *my*, *we*, and *our*.

Example
As soon as I walked into the room, I could tell something was wrong with my computer. I took off my coat and sat down.

Example
As soon as Maria and I walked into the room, we could tell something was wrong with our computer. I took off my coat and sat down.

Sometimes the narrator isn't a character in the story, but just someone looking in from the outside and reporting what happened. This is called the **third-person** point of view. The narrator uses words like *he, she, they,* and *their.*

Example

As soon as Maria and Mark walked into the room, they could tell something was wrong with their computer. She took off her coat, hung it up, and sat down.

There is a **second-person** point of view, but it's not used very often in literature. The narrator talks directly to a character in the story and uses words like *you* and *your*.

Example

As soon as you walk into the room, you can tell something is wrong with the computer. You take off your coat, hang it up, and sit down.

Literary works most commonly use either first- or third-person points of view. Using a second-person point of view to tell a story tends to get tiresome. So second-person is used more for giving directions, in personal letters, and sometimes in advertisements.

PRACTICE 1: *DRACULA*

Excerpted and adapted from the book by Bram Stoker

Read the selection, and then answer the questions that follow.

(1)   The carriage went at a hard pace straight along. Then we made a complete turn and went along another straight road. It seemed to me that we were simply going over and over the same ground again, so I took note of a landmark and found this was so. I would have liked to ask the driver what this meant, but I feared to do so. By-and-by, however, as I was curious to know how time was passing, I struck a match. By its flame, I looked at my watch. It was a few minutes until midnight.

(2)   Then a dog began to howl somewhere in a farmhouse far down the road. It was a long, agonized wailing, as if from fear. The sound was taken up by another dog, and then another and another. Borne on the wind now sighing softly through the Pass, a wild howling seemed to come from all over the country through the gloom of night. The horses began to strain and rear, but the driver quieted them down. Then, from the mountains on each side of us rose a louder, sharper howling. It was that of wolves, which affected both the horses and me in the same way.

1. The most likely narrator of this selection is
    a. the character who's driving the carriage.
    b. the character who owns the horses.
    c. the farmer whose dog is howling.
    d. the character who's riding in the carriage.

2. Which words in the first paragraph were clues to the point of view?
    a. they, driver, this
    b. we, I, my
    c. by, how, it
    d. it, its, this

3. This selection is told from
    a. a third-person point of view.
    b. a second-person point of view.
    c. a first-person point of view
    d. a fourth-person point of view.

PRACTICE 2: *THE FLIGHT OF ICARUS*

A Greek Myth Retold

Read the selection, and then answer the questions that follow.

(1) In ancient Greece lived Daedalus, a talented and clever builder. He created everything from palaces to playthings for the wealthy. One of his rich clients was Minos, the King of Crete, an island in the Mediterranean.

(2) Minos was thought to be the richest and most powerful ruler of his time. He hired Daedalus to design and build a special, intricate maze, or labyrinth, to hold the Minotaur. It was a terrifying half-bull, half-human creature with a great appetite for humans. Minos wanted the creature confined somewhere in the maze so that it couldn't escape and be a threat to his people.

(3) Daedalus designed a masterful, mysterious maze, and his young son Icarus helped him create it. When the maze was finished, Minos had his soldiers release the Minotaur into it. But Minos worried that someone might find a way through the maze to release the creature. He had to make sure no one else ever knew the secret of the maze. So, to guarantee that Daedalus or Icarus could never reveal the secret, Minos imprisoned them in a very high tower.

(4)   Daedalus looked around. The tower had no windows or doors from which to escape. Only the top of the tower was open, spreading a ceiling of sky above them. Through it, day-after-day, an archer sent arrows tied with packets of food and tiny wax candles to help them see at night. The walls were too high to climb. There was no way out!

(5)   But the brilliant Daedalus devised a plan. Over time he and Icarus ate very little and grew thinner and lighter. At night, they used only the light from the moon and stars, and saved the tiny candles. Daedalus and Icarus used the leftover food to attract some of the thousands of birds that migrated across the sky above them. They plucked a single feather from each bird that landed, knowing that one feather was not enough to stop them from flying.

(6)   Daedalus explained to Icarus how the candle wax would hold the feathers on their arms like wings. They waited for a perfect day, when strong winds blew from the south . . . strong enough to carry them north toward Athens. At last, that day arrived. As they prepared to leave, Daedalus warned Icarus not to fly too high. "The heat of the sun could melt the wax that holds your wing feathers in place," he warned.

(7)   Then the wind lifted Daedalus and Icarus off the tower and they soared like birds high above the maze. Icarus flew higher and higher, enjoying the thrill of flight so much that he forgot his father's advice. The higher he flew, the thinner the air, and soon he could hardly breathe. He was hot and confused. Perhaps the height affected his brain. The sun began to melt the wax that held the feathers on to his arms. Icarus flapped his arms but to no avail. He tumbled like a wounded bird into the sea. Only a few scattered feathers floated on the water. Daedalus mourned his son, then continued on to safety.

4. Who is the narrator of this passage?
   a. the character of Icarus
   b. the character of Daedalus
   c. a third person, not a character
   d. the character of Minos

5. Which sentence is written from the first-person point of view?
   a. The higher Icarus flew, the thinner the air, and soon he could hardly breathe.
   b. The higher I flew, the thinner the air, and soon I could hardly breathe.
   c. The higher you flew, the thinner the air, and soon you could hardly breathe.
   d. The higher he flew, the thinner the air, and soon Icarus could hardly breathe.

6. Which sentence is written from the second-person point of view?
   a. The higher Icarus flew, the thinner the air, and soon he could hardly breathe.
   b. The higher I flew, the thinner the air, and soon I could hardly breathe.
   c. The higher you flew, the thinner the air, and soon you could hardly breathe.
   d. The higher he flew, the thinner the air, and soon Icarus could hardly breathe.

7. Rewrite the second to last paragraph from the story in the first person, as if you were Daedalus.

 Daedalus explained to Icarus how the candle wax would hold the feathers on their arms like wings. They waited for a perfect day, when strong winds blew from the south . . . strong enough to carry them north toward Athens. At last, that day arrived. As they prepared to leave, Daedalus warned Icarus not to fly too high. "The heat of the sun could melt the wax that holds your wing feathers in place," he warned.

_____

_____

_____

_____

_____

PRACTICE 3: *A JOURNEY TO THE INTERIOR OF THE EARTH*

Excerpted and adapted from the novel by Jules Verne

Read the selection, and then answer the questions that follow.

(1) WEDNESDAY, AUGUST 19. Fortunately, the wind blows violently, and has enabled us to flee from the scene of the late terrible struggle. My uncle, Professor Liedenbrock, began again to look impatiently around him. The voyage resumes its natural tone.

(2) THURSDAY, AUGUST 20. About noon, a distant noise is heard. I note the fact without being able to explain it. It is a continuous roar. Three hours pass. The roarings seem to come from a very distant waterfall and I remark this to my uncle, who replies, "Axel, you may be right."

(3) Are we, then, speeding forward to some waterfall, which will throw us down an abyss? This method of getting to the center of the earth may please my uncle, but I prefer an ordinary horizontal movement. At any rate, now the roarings are increasingly louder. Do they come from the sky or the ocean? I look up. The sky is calm and motionless. I look out to the horizon, which is unbroken and clear of all mist. If the noise is coming from a waterfall and the ocean does flow headlong into a lower level, then the water would move faster as a sign of the danger ahead. I quickly observe the water. It moves at normal speed. I throw an empty bottle into the sea: It lies still in the water.

(4) Hans climbs the mast to look out across the sea and points to the south, saying: "Down there! I see a vast cone of water rising from the surface!"

(5) "Is it another sea beast?" I ask. "Then let us steer farther westward, for we know something of the danger of coming across monsters of that sort."

(6) "Let us go straight on, Axel," replies my uncle, calmly.

(7) The nearer we approach, the higher the jets of water. What monster could possibly fill itself with such a quantity of water, and spurt it up so continuously? By evening, we are close enough to see its body—dark, enormous, like a hill spread upon the sea as an island. Is it illusion or fear? Its length seems to me a couple of thousand yards!

(8) What can this creature be, that no explorer who came here before made note of? It lies motionless, as if asleep. The column of water it throws up to a height of five hundred feet falls in rain with a deafening uproar. And here we are, heading like lunatics to get near to a monster that a hundred whales a day would not satisfy!

8. This selection is told from
  a. a fourth-person point of view.
  b. a third-person point of view.
  c. a second-person point of view.
  d. a first-person point of view

9. The narrator of the story is
  a. Hans.
  ~~b. Axel.~~
  c. Professor Liedenbrock.
  d. the sea monster.

10. Which sentence is written from the second-person point of view?

    a. "Is it another sea beast?" I ask.

    b. "Is it another sea beast?" Hans asks.

    c. "Is it another sea beast?" you ask.

    d. "Is it another sea beast?" they ask.

11. If Hans were the narrator, the story would probably be different because

    a. he would tell what he personally saw, said, felt, and did.

    b. he would tell more about how Axel was feeling.

    c. it would be told from the third person point of view.

    d. it would be more about the kinds of foods they ate on the voyage.

12. Rewrite this second paragraph from the story in the third person. Remember to change any necessary verb endings.

    About noon, a distant noise is heard. I note the fact without being able to explain it. It is a continuous roar. Three hours pass. The roarings seem to come from a very distant waterfall and I remark this to my uncle, who replies, "Axel, you may be right."

ANSWERS

1. d
2. b
3. c
4. c
5. b
6. c
7. *I* explained to Icarus how the candle wax would hold the feathers on *our* arms like wings. *We* waited for a perfect day, when strong winds blew from the south . . . strong enough to carry *us* north toward Athens. At last, that day arrived. As *we* prepared to leave, *I* warned Icarus not to fly too high. "The heat of the sun could melt the wax that holds your wing feathers in place," *I* warned.
8. d
9. b
10. c
11. a
12. About noon, a distant noise is heard. *Axel* notes the fact without being able to explain it. It is a continuous roar. Three hours pass. The roarings seem to come from a very distant waterfall and *Axel* remarks this to *his* uncle, who replies, "Axel, you may be right."

theme

I stick to simple themes. Love. Hate. No nuances.
JOHN WAYNE (1907–1979)
AMERICAN MOVIE ACTOR

In this lesson, you'll discover how to find the overall message an author gives you in a selection.

THE THEME OF a story is the most important thing the author wants readers to understand. It's the author's thoughts about a general belief of how things are or how they should be. In fables, the theme is the moral, or lesson, the story teaches. The moral may even be stated at the end of the story. Remember that Aesop story about the Fox and Crow in Lesson 23? If the theme had been stated, it would have been something like this: *Don't be distracted by flattery or vain people can be easily fooled!*

Here are a few other familiar themes you'll find in stories.

STORY THEMES

Don't cry over spilled milk.
Believe in yourself.
Deeds speak louder than words.
Honesty is the best policy.
Justice for all.
Bad things sometimes happen to good people.
Don't envy others; be happy with what you have.
Money can't buy happiness.
Look before you leap.
To have a friend, you have to be a friend.
Don't believe everything you hear.
Beauty is only skin-deep.

An author may not state the theme directly, but you can figure it out. Think about what the characters in the story are like and what they do, and ask yourself questions like:

- Did something that happened in the story change a character?
- How do the characters' actions relate to things in my life?
- What message is the author trying to send me?
- Does the title of the story give a clue to the theme?

PRACTICE 1: "SEA FEVER"

by John Masefield

Read the selection, and then answer the questions that follow.

> I must down to the seas again, to the lonely sea and the sky,
> And all I ask is a tall ship and a star to steer her by,
> And the wheel's kick and the wind's song and the white sail's shaking,
> And a gray mist on the sea's face, and a gray dawn breaking.

I must down to the seas again, for the call of the running tide
Is a wild call and a clear call that may not be denied;
And all I ask is a windy day with the white clouds flying,
And the flung spray and the blown spume, and the sea-gulls crying.

I must down to the seas again, to the vagrant gypsy life,
To the gull's way and the whale's way, where the wind's like a whetted
    knife;
And all I ask is a merry yarn from a laughing fellow-rover,
And quiet sleep and a sweet dream when the long trick's over.

1. What is the theme, or message, the author expresses in this poem?
   a. Hard work never hurt anyone.
   b. The simple things in life may be the best.
   c. Everyone should learn to sail.
   d. There should be freedom for all people.

2. What words are repeated to point out the theme?
   a. and the
   b. to the seas
   c. all I ask
   d. I must down

3. In your own life, according to the theme, if you
   a. work harder, you can own your own boat.
   b. look around, you'll find simple things that make you happy.
   c. like the sea, you will be very happy on shore.
   d. don't have a hobby, you should get one.

PRACTICE 2: *EPAMINONDAS*

A Folk Tale Retold

Read the selection, and then answer the questions that follow.

(1)   Epaminondas lived with his mama in a little house on a hill. He was a
sweet boy, but as his mama always said, not the brightest bulb in the
lamp! Most days, Epaminondas went to visit his auntie. She lived on the
other side of the hill. He loved to walk through the forest and cross the
stream to her house. Most days she gave him something to take home.

(2) One day Auntie gave Epaminondas half a cake. He grabbed it in his fists and carried it home. When he got there, it was smeared all over his hands. "What have you got there?" asked Mama.

(3) "Cake, Mama," said Epaminondas.

(4) "Epaminondas, that's no way to carry cake!" said Mama. "You wrap it in clean leaves and put it in your hat. Now will you remember that?"

(5) "Yes, Mama," said Epaminondas.

(6) The next week, Auntie gave Epaminondas some fresh, sweet butter. He wrapped it in leaves and put it in his hat. It was a hot day. The butter began to melt and when he got home, it was all over him. His mama cried, "That's no way to carry butter! You wrap it in leaves, cool it in the brook, and carry it home! Will you remember that?"

(7) By and by, Auntie gave Epaminondas a puppy. He wrapped it in leaves, cooled it in the brook, and carried it home. His mama rubbed the poor shivering pup with a soft towel and fed it warm soup. "That's no way to treat a puppy!" she said. "You tie a string around its neck, put it on the ground, and walk it home! Will you remember?"

(8) "Yes, Mama," said Epaminondas.

(9) Today, Auntie gave Epaminondas a freshly-baked loaf of bread. He tied a string around it, put it on the ground, and walked home! The birds loved it because there were enough crumbs on the ground to feed a flock for a week! But when he got home, all he had left was a small, sticky lump of bread stuck to the string!

(10) His mama shook her head and said, "No sense telling you any more, Epaminondas! Now I'm going to get more bread from Auntie. You see those pies cooling on the porch? They're for the bake sale. While I'm gone, you *mind how you step in those pies!*"

(11) Now *we* know she meant "be careful and *don't* step in the pies," but Epaminondas *minded* his mama. He stepped right in the middle of each pie! When his mama got home and saw the mess, she just laughed. "Oh, Epaminondas, you ain't got the brains you were born with . . . but I love you anyway!" Then she gave him a big hug . . . and a slice of fresh bread.

4. Which best states the theme of this folk tale?
   a. Do things the right way the first time.
   b. Give unconditional love and accept differences in people.
   c. Always bring your own groceries home.
   d. Volunteer to help children visit their relatives.

5. Which character in the story most clearly states the author's message?
   a. Mama
   b. Epaminondas
   c. Auntie
   d. none of the above

6. Which would most likely have been the theme if Auntie had given Epaminondas a bag of money and he had lost it on the way home?
   a. You can't believe everything you hear!
   b. It's better to be safe than sorry.
   c. Slow and steady wins the race.
   d. Money can't buy happiness.

7. The most likely theme, if Auntie gave Epaminondas milk and he dropped it, is
   a. better late than never.
   b. don't cry over spilled milk.
   c. deeds speak louder than words.
   d. everyone has some kind of talent.

8. Which other word describes the theme of the Epaminondas story?
   a. compassion
   b. loathing
   c. panic
   d. prosperity

PRACTICE 5: *THE HARE AND THE TORTOISE*

An Aesop's Fable retold

Read the selection, and then answer the questions that follow.

(1) "I'm the fastest animal around!" Hare boasted to all the other animals. "I can run faster than anyone in the world!"

(2) "POOH!" Tortoise said with a sly smile. "Lots of us could beat you. Why, I could even beat you in a race."

(3) All the animals laughed. Some of them thought they might be able to beat Hare, but Tortoise? She was a slowpoke and always late, arriving just a little ahead of Snail, who was the slowest! Hare thought the whole idea so funny he fell down laughing. "You think you can beat ME?" he chuckled.

(4) "I KNOW I can!" replied Tortoise.

(5) "Okay," Hare said, "let's race from here to the lake right now!"

(6) Tortoise looked down the road. She was so short that she couldn't actually see the lake, but she knew how to get there.

(7) "Are we going to race or what?" Hare asked as he winked at the other animals.

(8) "Let's go!" replied Tortoise.

(9) "I'll start the race for you," said Goose. "When I honk, the race will begin."

(10) Tortoise and Hare stood very still. All was quiet. Then . . . HONK! Hare raced off, hopping down the road as fast as his legs would take him. Tortoise crawled away, lumbering down the road behind him as fast as her feet would go. When he was about halfway to the lake, Hare stopped and looked back. He could barely see the outline of Tortoise plodding along the road far behind. "Man, that Tortoise will never catch me!" he laughed. "I think I'll take a nap!" So he curled up under a big apple tree and before long, was fast asleep.

(11) When Hare finally awoke, he looked back down the road to see where Tortoise was. She was nowhere in sight. Then he looked ahead and couldn't believe his eyes! Tortoise was almost at the finish line! He jumped up and ran as fast as he could, but he was too late. He arrived just as Tortoise slowly crawled across the finish line, the winner.

(12) Amid cheers from the crowd, a smiling Tortoise said to Hare, "I may be slow, much slower than you, but I don't stop until I'm through. 'Cause no matter how hard a hill is to climb, slow and steady wins every time!"

9. According to the theme of this fable,
    a. it's important to take time out to nap.
    b. being a tortoise is much harder than being a goose.
    c. keep going and you'll reach your goal.
    d. it's important to win at any cost.

10. Which would most likely have been the theme if Tortoise had NOT won?
   a. You can do anything you set your mind to.
   b. Friendship is more important than anything.
   c. Slow and steady wins the race.
   d. Don't overestimate your own ability.

11. Which one word best describes the theme of the fable?
   a. recklessness
   b. perseverance
   c. admiration
   d. extravagance

12. The most likely theme, if Hare had started before the HONK, would be
   a. the early bird gets the worm.
   b. all is fair in love and war.
   c. keep your eye on the prize.
   d. winners never cheat and cheaters never win.

13. Which messages does the author also get across in the selection?
   a. Don't brag about how good you are at something.
   b. Don't take anything for granted.
   c. Think before you speak.
   d. all of the above

ANSWERS

   1. b
   2. c
   3. b
   4. b
   5. a
   6. d
   7. b
   8. a
   9. c
   10. d
   11. b
   12. d
   13. d

LESSON 27

imagery

In this lesson, you'll discover how authors choose words to create pictures in your mind.

IMAGERY IS THE use of words to help readers visualize, or create pictures in their minds, of people, places, and events in a story. Authors choose words that appeal to readers' five senses: sight, hearing, smell, taste, and touch. See the chart on the following page for some examples.

SIMPLE DESCRIPTION	USING IMAGERY
Marta saw tulips in the garden.	Marta spied one bright yellow tulip peeking its head above the others.
I heard the horn of a car as it came my way.	I was interrupted by the shrill blast of a horn as a car rushed toward me and screeched to a stop.
We had to walk through the rain.	We sloshed through the puddles as cold, bone-chilling rain poured down harder and harder.
In the kitchen, I smelled bacon and onions.	As I came into the kitchen, I noted a strong, sharp odor of onions and the lingering fumes from frying bacon. My mouth watered!
We bought some popcorn to eat at the movie.	Lee carried the large bucket of fluffy, crunchy, butter-dripping popcorn for us to share as we watched the show.

Visualizing helps you connect with the text by picturing things you already know. That, in turn, helps you better remember what you read. A word web like this one can help you organize details as you visualize characters, settings, or events.

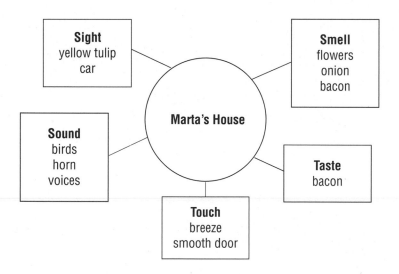

PRACTICE 1: LONE SHADOW'S ADVENTURE

Read the selection, and then answer the questions that follow.

(1)   It's quiet on the prairie. The only thing Lone Shadow can hear is the beating of his heart. A few butterflies silently swoop down to rest on tall grasses that spread out as far as the eye can see. Above, a few fluffy white clouds float in an endless blue sky. A gentle breeze drifts past Lone Shadow's ear. Suddenly, there's movement in the grass ahead!

(2)   A frightened deer leaps past Lone Shadow's shoulder and races off toward a small clump of trees. Then he hears it . . . a rhythmic sound like his heartbeat, only louder! The ground begins to tremble. He looks toward the horizon and sees a swirling cloud of dust heading his way! Quickly he turns and runs. The noise gets louder and the dust thicker, so thick he can taste it! Just as he jumps into a deep ditch, a thundering herd of buffalo rushes past.

(3)   Once the herd has moved on, Lone Shadow walks to the place where he had been standing. There's a musty smell in the air above the grass, which is now flat. "That could have been me!" he says. Quickly he runs back to camp to tell the tribal leaders about the buffalo. . . . There will be a hunt tonight!

1. How did the author use sensory words to help readers visualize the character, setting, and events? Give at least one example from the text for each sense.

Sight_____

Hearing _____

Touch _____

Smell _____

Taste_____

2. Read this sentence from the text: *Suddenly, there's movement in the grass ahead!* Which of the following best adds imagery to help readers visualize the situation?

   a. Suddenly, there's some kind of movement somewhere in the grass ahead!

   b. Suddenly, Lone Shadow sees a flash of brown and white fur and hears something panting in the grass ahead!

   c. Suddenly, Lone Shadow sees an animal moving in the grass ahead!

   d. Suddenly, the grass ahead begins to bend. . . . Something is moving it!

PRACTICE 2: *THE UGLY DUCKLING*

Excerpted and adapted from a story by Hans Christian Andersen

Read the selection, and then answer the questions that follow.

(1)   It was lovely summer weather in the country. The yellow corn, green oats, and golden haystacks in the meadows looked beautiful. The stork walking about on his long red legs, chattered in the Egyptian language that he had learned from his mother. The cornfields and meadows were surrounded by large forests with large brown tree trunks topped with green leaves and bright blossoms. In the midst of the forests were deep pools of clear, sapphire water.

(2)   Beside the forests was a river, and close by stood a pleasant old farmhouse. From the house, one could see down to the water, where great thistles grew so high that under the tallest dark green leaves, a small child could stand upright! This wild, secluded spot formed a snug retreat in which a duck sat on a nest, waiting for her young brood to hatch.

(3)   The duck was beginning to tire of her task, for the little ones were a long time coming out of their shells, and she seldom had any visitors. The other ducks much preferred swimming in the river than climbing the slippery banks to sit under a thistle leaf and talk with her. She shifted on the itchy twigs of her nest. Finally, she heard one shell crack, and then another and another, and from each came a fuzzy creature that lifted its head and cried, "Peep, peep!"

(4) "Quack, quack," said the mother as she stroked each soft, yellow duckling. They looked about them on every side at the large green leaves. Their mother allowed them to look as much as they liked, because green is good for the eyes. "How large the world is," said the young ducks, when they found how much more room they had now than while inside their white eggshells.

(5) "Do you imagine this is the whole world?" laughed their mother. "Wait till you have seen the garden; it stretches far beyond that field, but I have never ventured such a distance. Are you all out?" she continued, rising. "No, the largest egg lies there still! I wonder how long this is to last; I am quite tired of it!" Then she fluffed her feathers and seated herself again on the nest.

3. How does the author help readers "visualize" the stork?
    a. by telling about its nest and what its eating
    b. by telling about the color of its feathers and eyes
    c. by telling the size and color of its legs and how it's talking
    d. by telling what it does when it sees the duck

4. How does the author help readers visualize the meadow?
    a. by explaining how each of the buildings is used
    b. by describing the colors of plants and other things
    c. by telling how old the trees are
    d. by describing all the fish

5. Read this sentence from the text: *It was lovely summer weather in the country.* Which of the following best adds imagery to help readers visualize the setting?
    a. It was lovely warm summer weather in the country.
    b. It was a warm, summer day and the sun's rays bathed the countryside in a soft, golden light.
    c. It was nice summer weather with plenty of sunshine all over the country.
    d. It was a hot summer day, so hot that the city streets were steaming.

6. Read this sentence from the text: *Beside the forests was a river, and close by stood a pleasant old farmhouse.* Which of the following best adds imagery to help readers visualize the place?
   a. Beside the trees runs a river, and not far away is an old farmhouse.
   b. Beside the forests of trees was a long river, and close by the river there was a nice but old farmhouse.
   c. A bubbling river raced beside the forests, spilling its liquid over smooth white rocks below a steep hill on which sat an old abandoned, red farmhouse.
   d. Along the sides of the forests was a rocky river, and further down the path there was an old white farmhouse.

7. What sounds does the author use to appeal to readers' sense of hearing?
   a. cracking of the eggs
   b. peeping of the ducklings
   c. quacking of the mother duck
   d. all of the above

8. How did the author appeal to the readers' sense of touch? Give examples from the text to support your ideas.

   _____

   _____

   _____

PRACTICE 3: *STORY OF MY LIFE*

Excerpted and adapted from the autobiography of Helen Keller

Read the selection, and then answer the questions that follow.

(1)   *Helen Keller was born in Alabama in 1880. A childhood illness left her blind and deaf, living in a silent, dark world where she often had frightening fits of anger. Then Anne Sullivan came to be her teacher. Helen not only learned to read, she graduated from college and was an active author and lecturer until her death in 1968. The following is from her autobiography.*

(2)   I lived, up to the time of the illness, in a tiny house consisting of a large square room and a small one, in which the servant slept. It is a custom in the South to build a small house near the family home as an addition to be used on occasion. Such a house my father built after the Civil War, and when he married my mother they went to live in it.

(3)   The little house was completely covered with vines, climbing roses and honeysuckles. It was a favorite meeting place for hummingbirds and bees. The Keller main house, where the family lived, was a few steps from our little one. The homestead was called "Ivy Green" because the house and the surrounding trees and fences were covered with beautiful English ivy. The old-fashioned garden was the paradise of my childhood.

(4)   Even in the days before my teacher came, I used to feel along the square stiff boxwood hedges, and, guided by the sense of smell, would find the first violets and lilies in the garden. There, too, after a fit of temper, I went to find comfort and to hide my hot face in the cool leaves and grass. What joy it was to lose myself in that garden, to wander happily until, coming upon a beautiful vine, I recognized it by its leaves and blossoms, and knew it covered the tumble-down summer house at the farther end of the garden! Here, also, were rare sweet flowers called butterfly lilies, because their fragile petals resemble butterflies' wings. But the roses—they were loveliest of all. Never have I found since such roses as those that hung from our porch. They filled the air with fragrance, and in the early morning, all washed by dew, they felt so soft.

(5)   They tell me I walked the day I was a year old. I was suddenly attracted by the flickering shadows of leaves that danced in the sunlight on the smooth floor. But these happy days did not last long. One brief spring, filled with the music of robins and mockingbirds, one summer rich in fruit and roses, one autumn of gold and crimson, sped by and left their gifts at the feet of a delighted child.

(6)   Then, in the dreary month of February, came the illness, which closed my eyes and ears and plunged me into the unconsciousness of a newborn baby. The doctor thought I could not live. But early one morning, the fever left me as suddenly and mysteriously as it had come. There was great rejoicing in the family that morning. But no one, not even the doctor, knew that I should never see or hear again.

9. How does the author use imagery to help readers "see" her?
   a. by telling when her father built the house and when he and her mother moved into it
   b. by describing the first time she walked, how she hid when she was angry, and how she felt her way along the hedges
   c. by describing the furniture in the two rooms of the house and where she ate her meals
   d. by telling what Anne Sullivan looked like and how she taught Helen to read

10. How did the author use sensory words to help readers visualize the setting and events in her life? Give at least two examples from the text for each sense listed.

Sight _____

Hearing _____

Touch _____

Smell _____

11. How does the author use imagery to help readers understand what it must be like to be unable to hear or see?
   a. by mentioning that a teacher came to help her
   b. by comparing it to the unconsciousness of a newborn baby
   c. by comparing the garden to when she learned to walk
   d. by telling about hearing the mockingbird sing

ANSWERS

1. You should have at least one of these: *Sight*—tall grass, white clouds, blue sky, butterflies, deer, clump of trees, cloud of dust, buffalo, flattened grass. *Hearing*—beating heart, thunder of hoofs, Lone Shadow's voice. *Touch*—breeze, frightened deer brushing shoulder. *Smell*—musty. *Taste*—dust
2. b
3. c
4. b
5. b
6. c
7. d
8. slippery, itchy, fizzy, soft, fluffed
9. b
10. You should have at least two of these: *Sight*—tiny, square, small, leaves, grass, vines, roses, honeysuckles, hummingbirds, bees, ivy, trees, fences, hedges, tumble-down summer house, butterfly wings, flickering shadows, sunlight, fruit, gold, crimson. *Hearing*—humming of hummingbirds, music of robins and mockingbirds. *Touch*—stiff, temper (anger), hot, cool, fragile petals, wet dew, soft, smooth, dreary. *Smell*—violets, lilies, fragrance of roses, sweet butterfly lilies
11. b

flashback and foreshadowing

The future is an unknown, but a somewhat predictable unknown.
To look to the future we must first look back upon the past.
ALBERT EINSTEIN (1879–1955)
GERMAN-BORN SCIENTIST

In this lesson, you'll find that sometimes authors want you to know what happened before . . . or what's going to happen later!

FLASHBACKS INTERRUPT WHAT'S going on in a story to tell about something that happened in the past. Authors use words like "He remembered when . . ." or "She thought about that time last year when . . ." Authors sometimes signal when the flashback is over by using words like *Now* or *Today*. A flashback gives readers a deeper understanding of a character's personality.

Example
"You're getting it. Good girl!" Anya cheered as she ran beside her little sister. Anya smiled, remembering when her dad had taught her to ride a bike. She could still see him running beside her, even when he didn't need to anymore! He'd always been so protective. But now, he was gone and she alone had to take care of the family. "I still need you, Dad," she whispered.

Flashbacks can give you information about a character to help you figure out his or her motives, or reasons, for doing things. This example would help you understand why Anya might turn down a chance to travel with a band, even though that was her dream.

Foreshadowing gives readers clues about what might happen later in a story. Authors use foreshadowing to build suspense, tempt readers to predict what might happen, and persuade them to read on to find out if they were right. Think about it. Even as a little kid, no one had to tell you that when Mrs. Rabbit told Peter, "Don't go into Mr. MacGregor's garden," he'd go . . . and get into trouble! The author's words foreshadowed danger.

Example
I looked at the speedometer. . . . Paul was driving even faster. "Please slow down," I said. "We're coming to a really bad curve in the road!" But he didn't slow down and the snow was drifting higher and higher. I could hardly see the road!

Foreshadowing also "sets up" future events so you're prepared for them and they make sense. You don't know why the author mentions snowdrifts until later in the story, when the car hits a snowdrift that stops the vehicle from going over a cliff!

PRACTICE 1: *THE GRASSHOPPER AND THE ANT*

An Aesop's Fable Retold

Read the selection, and then answer the questions that follow.

(1)   One fine summer day, Grasshopper was hopping about in the field. As he chirped and danced, he spied Ant carrying a big kernel of corn to his nest. Grasshopper watched as Ant came back, lifted another kernel, then carried it to the nest as well. This happened repeatedly. Finally, Grasshopper asked, "Ant, why do you work so hard on such a lovely day?"

(2)   "Soon it will be winter," replied Ant. "I'm gathering food for my family. I suggest you do the same!"

(3)   "Why bother about winter?" asked Grasshopper. "There's plenty of food in the fields now!"

(4)   Ant remembered last winter and how deep snow had covered everything. There had been no way to get out of his anthill, let alone try to find food! Now, an even worse winter was predicted. "You'll feel differently when the big snow comes!" said Ant, as he shook his head and walked away.

(5)   When winter came, Grasshopper had no food. The fields were covered with deep snow. Grasshopper was very hungry and sad, knowing that Ant had food enough because he had worked hard to prepare in advance.

1. In this fable, the author uses flashback to have
  a. Grasshopper remember a song he used to sing.
  b. Ant remember where Grasshopper used to live.
  c. Ant remember how bad last winter was.
  d. Grasshopper remember where he hid seeds during the summer.

2. Which best foreshadowed what might happen in the story?
  a. Grasshopper hopped about in the field.
  b. An even worse winter was predicted.
  c. Ant walked away.
  d. Grasshopper chirped.

3. Based on the story, which do you predict could NOT happen?
  a. Grasshopper begs Ant for just a small bit of food.
  b. Ant feels sorry for Grasshopper and gives him food.
  c. Grasshopper digs under the snow and finds lots of food.
  d. Grasshopper gets weaker without any food.

PRACTICE 2: *THE FALL OF THE HOUSE OF USHER*

Excerpted and adapted from the story by Edgar Allan Poe

Read the selection, and then answer the questions that follow.

(1)   During a dull, dark, and soundless day in autumn, I was passing alone, on horseback, through a dreary tract of country. At length I found myself within view of the melancholy House of Usher. With the first glimpse of the building, a sense of insufferable gloom spread through me. I looked upon the house and its bleak walls with vacant eye-like windows and a few white trunks of decayed trees with utter depression. What was it, I paused to think, that so unnerved me about the House of Usher?

(2)   I reined my horse to the steep brink of a black mirror-like mountain lake that lay by the house. I looked down with a shudder upon the inverted images of the gray marsh plants, ghastly tree stems, and vacant eye-like windows. Nevertheless, in this gloomy mansion I intended to spend some weeks. Its owner, Roderick Usher, had been one of my close companions in boyhood, but many years had elapsed since our last meeting.

(3)   I called to mind the letter I had lately received from Roderick that indicated an uneasiness. He had spoken of an illness, a mental disorder, that depressed him. He also expressed an earnest hope that if he were to see me, his best friend, it would both cheer him up and improve his health. It had been his straightforward manner and truthfulness about the situation that compelled me to honor his request without hesitation.

(4)   As boys, we had been even closer, yet I knew very little of my friend. He had always been quite shy and not forthcoming about his situation. I was, of course, aware that for generations his family had been noted for its somewhat peculiar temperament and involvement in the arts, although more often the unusual rather than the typical styles of art and music. I had learned, too, that in the minds of the peasantry, over the centuries, the family had always been thought a bit strange. According to the local people, both the mansion and the family were referred to as "The House of Usher."

(5)   Now, I was here, looking down into the mountain pool. I again lifted my eyes to the house itself from its image in the pool, and scanned the building more closely.

(6)   The years of weather had discolored the stonework. Minute molds overspread the exterior, hanging from the masonry in a fine tangled web. No portion of the walls had fallen but there was a great inconsistency between the overall look and the crumbling condition of individual stones. It reminded me of old woodwork that rots for many years, with no breakage. Perhaps the eye of a more observant person might have seen a barely visible split, which extended from the front roof of the building down the wall in a zigzag direction, until it became lost in the dark waters of the mountain pool! I, obviously, did not!

4. In this selection, the author uses flashback to have the narrator
   a. remember a similar house where he had grown up.
   b. recall what was in a letter he had received.
   c. recall how he had almost drowned in a mountain pool.
   d. remember when he had visited Roderick in the hospital.

5. The author also uses flashback to have the narrator explain
   a. what the local people thought of Roderick's family.
   b. what kinds of games he and Roderick used to play as children.
   c. how long it took for Roderick's family to built the old house.
   d. where Roderick's mother and father were.

6. Which of these is NOT an example of foreshadowing in the selection?
   a. a sense of insufferable gloom
   b. the steep brink of a lake
   c. gray marsh plants
   d. a barely visible split in the wall

7. Which do you predict best foreshadows what might happen later in the story?
   a. that it's an autumn day
   b. that the windows look like eyes
   c. that the side of the house has a split
   d. that the narrator's riding a horse

8. Based on the selection, which do you predict could NOT happen?
   a. The narrator finds that Roderick is sick and needs his help.
   b. The narrator finds things inside the House of Usher as creepy as on the outside!
   c. The narrator worries about his own safety in the House of Usher.
   d. The narrator has a pleasant, uneventful stay at the House of Usher.

PRACTICE 3: SIGNS OF THE TIMES

Read the selection, and then answer the questions that follow.

(1)   "It's going to be one of those days," Marek thought to himself as he looked up at the board labeled DEPARTURES. His flight was delayed. He thought back to how the day had begun. When he woke up, the sun had been shining brightly and robins that had built a nest outside his window were chirping loudly. He'd jumped out of bed, anxious to start the first day of his vacation. But he'd tripped over the clothes he'd carelessly dropped on the floor the night before and banged his knee on the closet door.

(2)   Now he sat at the airport thinking, *"I guess I should have known this morning! Maybe it was an omen."* He wasn't exactly sure what an omen was, but his mom always said that when things went wrong, so he figured it fit! He pulled his cell from his backpack. Quickly, he sent a text to his mom at work, alerting her that although he should be in the air on the way to his dad's place in Florida, he hadn't left the ground. Next, he sent a message to his dad, so he wouldn't be waiting at the airport in Florida for a flight that didn't come.

(3)   When he was finished, Marek went to look for something to eat. He thought about the last time he'd gone on vacation with both Mom and Dad. They'd gone to that new theme park and had a great time. That had been the last time Dad had taken any real time off. . . . Mom insisted he worked too much. Then things changed, and now he was caught between two homes . . . the one he shared with Mom and the one we visited to see Dad.

(4)   Marek looked out the window and saw that everything was covered in a thick blanket of fog! Just then, he heard an announcement: "Due to the fog, all flights are delayed." *Could this be another omen?* he wondered.

(5)   For hours, Marek and the other passengers waited for news. The fog remained. No flights. Then Marek heard his cell. It was his dad. "Listen, you're still stuck up there and now they're forecasting a hurricane down here. I want you to have a great vacation, so why don't I come up there? . . . We can spend some time together, then fly here together next week. I can grab a flight now. . . . They say by the time we get up there, the fog will have lifted and we can land. What do you think?"

(6)   "I think it would be great, Dad!" Marek replied, wondering what Mom would think. "Can't wait to see you!"

(7)   Marek called his mom, relaying the change in plans. She told him to stay at the airport and she'd come to pick him . . . and his dad . . . up. Slowly, the fog lifted, and was totally gone when his dad landed and his mom picked them up.

(8)   On the way home, Marek noticed that Mom seemed happy to see Dad . . . and he seemed happy to see her. They laughed and talked about "the old days" all the way home. *"Maybe Dad was supposed to come here instead of me going there . . . maybe this whole thing was an omen. Could it mean they'll get back together?"* Marek wondered.

9. The author uses flashback to have Marek
   a. remember when he and his mother moved into the house.
   b. recall that his father had been a champion swimmer.
   c. recall when he tripped over his clothes that morning.
   d. remember where he had hidden his old suitcase.

10. The author also uses flashback to have Marek explain
    a. why he likes Florida better than the place where he lives.
    b. what his life had been like before his mom and sad split up.
    c. how the airports had changed since the last time he was there.
    d. why he didn't like hamburgers.

11. Which best foreshadows that something important would happen later in the story?
    a. Marek tripping over his clothes
    b. Marek hearing the birds chirping
    c. the foggy skies
    d. Mom being at work

12. Which foreshadows that Marek will discover that his dad has changed?
    a. Dad offers to take days off work to spend with Marek.
    b. Marek goes to find something to eat.
    c. Dad once took the family to a theme park.
    d. It's the first day of Marek's vacation.

ANSWERS

1. c
2. b
3. c
4. b
5. a
6. c
7. c
8. d
9. c
10. b
11. c
12. a

figurative language: idiom, personification, hyperbole

> *It's a strange world of language in which skating*
> *on thin ice can get you into hot water.*
> FRANKLIN P. JONES (1853–1935)
> AMERICAN HUMORIST

In this lesson, you'll discover three special ways authors use words to add interest to their stories.

AS YOU KNOW, authors use words to help readers create images in their minds. Most words are literal—they mean what they say. But sometimes authors use more creative, or figurative, language, like idioms, personification, and hyperbole.

An **idiom** is a group of words that doesn't mean exactly what it says.

Example
"That homework we had last night was a piece of cake!" Bill said.

Does Bill mean that the teacher handed out cake for the class to eat as homework? No, of course not. "A piece of cake" means the task was easy. Look for content clues to help you figure out the meanings of idioms.

Idiom	Meaning
She feels *down in the dumps*.	She feels sad, unhappy, discouraged.
When I told them, they were *all ears*!	They paid attention and listened.
Don't be such *a couch potato*!	Don't be lazy, inactive.
Don't *let the cat out of the bag*!	Don't tell the secret.
Wow, that was *a close shave*!	A narrow escape; almost got caught.
She has a *chip on her shoulder*!	Is resentful, holds a grudge.

Personification gives human qualities to animals or objects.

Example
"I cannot see in this tall grass, Moon," cried the tiger. So Moon smiled down while Wind puffed her cheeks and blew the grass aside.

In this example, the tiger has the human ability to speak, the Moon can smile, and the Wind has human-like cheeks and a mouth. Readers relate to the actions because they share the qualities. Personification adds interest to some stories, especially fables and myths that teach lessons about life and human behavior.

    Hyperbole is the use of exaggeration to make a point.

Example
"This suitcase weighs a ton!" Ray grumbled. "No wonder my back hurts!"

Does the suitcase really weigh a ton? Not likely, since a ton is 2,000 pounds! But the author wants to make the point that the suitcase is really heavy. Don't you wonder what's in it? The author hopes you do!

PRACTICE 1: *PAUL BUNYAN AND THE BIG JAM*

A Legend Retold

Read the selection, and then answer the questions that follow.

(1)   Folks say that one spring, the lumberjacks up North had cut down so many trees that there was the biggest logjam ever seen. There must have been a zillion logs crammed together 200 feet high by the bend of the river! The loggers chopped, sawed, and tugged at the wood, but they couldn't budge that jam one inch. That's when the call went out to get Paul Bunyan, the greatest logger who ever lived.

(2)   It was raining cats and dogs as Paul and his faithful Blue Ox, Babe, arrived. Suddenly the rain stopped and Paul led Babe to the front of the huge log pile. "You stay here," Paul said. "Okay," Babe replied with a nod of her head. Then Paul took a slingshot and fired bits of feathers at Babe, who thought she was being attacked by pesky flies. Babe began to swish her big old tail back and forth. It stirred up the river so much that the water turned and flowed upstream, taking the logs with it! The giant jam was broken! When Paul called Babe out of the water, the logs turned again and began to float back downstream to the mill!

1. The idiom *raining cats and dogs* means
  a. toy puppies and kittens fell from the sky.
  b. it was raining very hard.
  c. the message was sent quickly.
  d. people were talking very fast.

2. The author uses personification by
  a. making the river water go upstream.
  b. saying the loggers called for Paul Bunyan.
  c. having Paul talk to Babe.
  d. having Babe talk to Paul.

3. Which is an example of hyperbole?
  a. swish her big old tail
  b. couldn't budge that jam one inch
  c. there must have been a zillion logs
  d. attacked by pesky flies

PRACTICE 2: LETTER TO A FRIEND

Read the selection, and then answer the questions that follow.

Hey, Jen,

(1)   Hope you're not burning the midnight oil studying. I sure wish you were here. I can't believe our schools got their wires crossed this year and we have different vacation schedules! It seems unreal being on this trip without you and your family. Frankly, it's the worst vacation anyone ever had!

(2)   I was really feeling down in the dumps this morning, so Mom suggested I go shopping. No kidding! At home, I have to ask her at least a million times before she lets me head off to the mall! Well, there isn't any mall near here, but there is this cool local street market. You can find everything there from footwear to fossils! There are colorful tents set up all up and down the streets, and the most delicious smells of different kinds of foods invite you to get closer.

(3)   Just walking around the market, I was so hungry I could have eaten a horse! I tried everything . . . I think the sellers knew they'd found a real tourist! I bought lots of cool stuff. . . . At first the sellers try to charge an arm and a leg, but you can negotiate for a better price. I got some real bargains. . . . You'll see when we get home. Don't worry; I remembered to pick out something special for you. I bought so much I thought I'd need a pickup truck to get it all back to the hotel!

(4)   As I passed this one tent, a wacky yellow hat called to me. . . . I could almost hear it screaming, "Buy me! Buy me!" So I did. That hat was awesome. The seller said it was one-of-a-kind. It had this intricate beaded work and Mom thinks there are semiprecious stones and ostrich feathers on it, too. All I know is, I figured everyone would get a kick out of it when I wore it to school. But just then, up comes this storm. The wind starts to howl, stretches out its icy fingers, and grabs the hat right off my head! My new hat tumbled over and over across the ground, with me in hot pursuit. Just when I'd reached it, off it would tumble. Finally, a big gust of wind blew it totally out of sight. The bottom line is, my fabulous hat is gone forever. I tried to find another, but no luck. Sorry you'll never have a chance to see it. . . . It really was special.

(5)   Well, hey, Mom just popped in and says we have to get going. There's some kind of dinner thing. . . . Sure hope they have some good old American food.

(6)   Say "Hi" to your family from Mom and me.

       Pat

4. Which is NOT an idiom?
   a. got their wires crossed
   b. feeling down in the dumps
   c. isn't any mall near here
   d. get a kick out of it

5. In the selection, the idiom *burning the midnight oil* means
   a. going to a gas station late at night.
   b. staying up late at night to do homework.
   c. sitting in front of a fireplace.
   d. sleeping until well past noon.

6. One use of personification in the selection was when
   a. the market was filled with delicious smells.
   b. Pat's mom suggested going to the street market.
   c. the hat called out to Pat.
   d. Pat hoped there would be American food.

7. The author used personification to give human-like fingers to the
   a. letter.
   b. tents.
   c. hat.
   d. wind.

8. Which is an example of hyperbole?
   a. a big gust of wind
   b. had this intricate beaded work
   c. need a pickup truck to get it all back
   d. got some real bargains

9. *I could have eaten a horse* is hyperbole that means
   a. I needed something . . . anything, to eat.
   b. I was too tired to walk anymore.
   c. I had too much to eat.
   d. I was too sleepy to eat anything at all.

PRACTICE 3: *THE BAT, THE BIRDS, AND THE BEASTS*

An Aesop's Fable Retold

Read the selection, and then answer the questions that follow.

(1)   Once, about a quadrillion years ago, the Birds and the Beasts of the earth
prepared for a great war. No one knows exactly who started the war; it just
happened. There were rumors that one of the winged creatures got a bit
bent out of shape and said something that rubbed one of the Beasts the
wrong way! Whatever the reason, the day and time for battle were set.

(2) The winged creatures flew to the meeting place. On the way, they passed Bat, who was perched in a tree. "Come with us!" they called to Bat. "You are a winged creature, too!"

(3) Bat looked at the other flying creatures. He did not want to fight at all, so he said, "No, I can't join you!"

(4) "Why not?" asked a gruff vulture that was as big as a house!

(5) "Please, don't jump all over me!" Bat replied as he pointed to his sharp teeth. "I can't join you because I'm . . . a Beast!"

(6) The winged creatures just shrugged their shoulders and moved on.

(7) Later, the Beasts walked by. "Come with us!" called one Beast who had feet the size of logs! "You're a Beast, like us. Come and help us fight!"

(8) Bat didn't beat around the bush; he just fluttered his wings and said, "I hate to blow my own horn here, friends, but can't you see I am a Bird?"

(9) The Beasts just shook their heads and marched away.

(10) Later that day, representatives from the Birds and the Beasts met to talk things over. Luckily, a peace treaty was negotiated and there was no battle. Instead, each side had its own feast of celebration.

(11) Bat saw that there were parties going on and wanted to join the fun. First, he went to the Birds' party, but they flew at him and chased him away. "You have sharp teeth so you're not a Bird!" they cried. "This party is for Birds only!"

(12) Then Bat went to join the Beasts, but had to fly away before they tore him apart! "You have wings, so you must be a Bird," they cried. "This party is for Beasts only!"

(13) High in the tree, Bat watched the celebrations and said sadly, "If you don't claim to be one thing or the other, you have no friends!" Since then, the friendless Bat hides from other creatures in caves by day, and hunts only in the dark of night.

10. Personification is used in this fable to
   a. make humans do things that animals do.
   b. have animals talk and act like humans.
   c. have the Beasts play like humans in a rock band.
   d. make the Bat use human-like arms to row a boat to a desert island.

11. What is the meaning of the idiom *get bent out of shape*?
- **a.** Get plenty of exercise.
- **b.** Reverse direction.
- **c.** Get upset or angry.
- **d.** Buy a pretzel.

12. Which is NOT an idiom?
- **a.** rub one the wrong way
- **b.** blow my own horn
- **c.** beat around the bush
- **d.** shrug their shoulders and moved on

13. Which is an example of hyperbole?
- **a.** a gruff vulture
- **b.** as big as a house
- **c.** perched in a tree
- **d.** feast of celebration

14. The author uses the hyperbole *feet the size of logs* to help readers
- **a.** visualize an animal with really long feet.
- **b.** visualize an animal that would make squeaking sounds.
- **c.** visualize an animal with very long hair.
- **d.** visualize an animal sitting on a log.

ANSWERS

1. b
2. d
3. c
4. c
5. b
6. c
7. d
8. c
9. a
10. b
11. c
12. d
13. b
14. a

figurative language: similes and metaphors

An idea is a feat of association, and the height of it is a good metaphor.
ROBERT FROST (1874–1963)
AMERICAN POET

In this lesson, you'll discover two more ways authors use specific words to add interest to their writing.

SIMILES AND METAPHORS are two more kinds of figurative language that authors use to add interest to their writing.

A **simile** compares two things by using the words *like* or *as*.

Example
I was so embarrassed; my face was as red as a beet!

How can the author compare a person's face to a vegetable? They're so different! True, but they are alike in one way: Both are red. Picturing this can help you visualize the character and understand his or her motives in a story.

Here are few more similes. What do they help you visualize?

You and I are as alike as two peas in a pod!

She is as quiet as a mouse.

His sadness was as unending as the waves crashing on shore.

I know I can trust him; he's as honest as the day is long.

I can't get her to do anything; she's as stubborn as a mule!

A **metaphor** compares two things without using *like* or *as*. The text states that one thing is, or has the characteristics of, another.

Example
The dog's eyes were searchlights, looking for any sign of kindness.

Is the author tying to get you to picture a dog with huge searchlights for eyes? No, the author wants you to visualize a poor dog staring intently, looking for kindness from a stranger.

Here are a few more metaphors. What do you visualize with each?

Night is a curtain that eventually falls.

The quarterback is a well-maintained machine.

She is a beacon of light, guiding us home.

Strength and honor are his uniform.

Silence is an invited guest, allowing me time to think.

PRACTICE 1: WORD RHYMES

Here are three very short four-line rhymes that contain similes and metaphors. Read each, and then answer the questions that follow.

The breeze is a messenger,
As sweet as roses in bloom,
That fills all the corners
Of my lonely room.

The sky is a blanket
Bejeweled with diamonds so bright
That twinkle and sparkle
Like fireflies at night.

The street is a river
On which traffic can flow
Where cars scurry like fish
And swish to and fro.

1. In the first rhyme, the author uses a simile to compare a
  a. fish to the scent of a rose.
  b. breeze to the sweet smell of roses.
  c. messenger to a lonely room.
  d. lonely room to a windstorm.

2. Which of these is NOT a metaphor?
  a. The breeze is a messenger.
  b. The sky is a blanket.
  c. like fireflies at night
  d. The street is a river.

3. How does the author use a simile in the last rhyme?
  a. to compare the street to a river
  b. to compare cars to fish
  c. to compare stars to fireflies
  d. to compare roses to traffic

PRACTICE 2: *ATALANTA AND THE FINAL RACE*

A Greek Myth Retold

Read the selection, and then answer the questions that follow.

(1) Long ago, there lived in Greece a beautiful princess by the name of Atalanta. She was a swift runner . . . as fast as lightning, they say. In fact, she was the fastest person in the kingdom. Whenever she ran down a mountain path, she was the wind that moved the trees.

(2) When Atalanta reached the age when most girls were married, her father decided that she, too, should marry. To Atalanta, that idea was about as welcome as a skunk at an outdoor party! She didn't want to marry anyone yet. So at first, she was mad as a wet hen. "But Daughter," said her father, "you are the sun in my sky. I just want you to find someone who will make you happy."

(3) Now Atalanta was as cunning as a fox, so she said, in a voice as sweet as honey. "I know you want the best for me, Father, so I will marry the man who can beat me in a foot race!"

(4) Of course, Atalanta was sure she could beat any man, so she wouldn't have to marry . . . until she was ready. The king sent out the word: Any man who could beat the princess in a running race would win her hand in marriage.

(5) Many young men came to try their luck. Atalanta took them on, one at a time. Each competitor was given a head start, but since she was faster than a speeding bullet, Atalanta won each race! Then one day a handsome prince named Hippomenes came to the castle. He took one look at Atalanta and fell in love. Although she was as cold as ice to him, he was determined to win the race and marry her.

(6) Aphrodite, the goddess of love, helped Hippomenes. "Take these three lovely golden apples that shine like the stars," she said. "Find some way to use them wisely during the race to win your true love."

(7) The next morning, Hippomenes and Atalanta waited at the starting line. She offered him a head start, and he took off like a rocket. Before Atalanta could overtake him, Hippomenes threw a golden apple on the path in front of her. When she spotted the apple, Atalanta couldn't resist stopping to pick it up. Then on she ran, almost catching up, but then he threw the second apple. Again, she stopped to pick it up, then ran on. Hippomenes threw the last apple so far off the path that by the time Atalanta picked it up, it was impossible for her to catch up. He crossed the finish line a split second before her.

(8) Atalanta congratulated her opponent. He smiled and winked, and suddenly she realized that she'd been tricked. But she was not angry for she also realized that he was a very clever man and could run very fast . . . two things she admired. "You are very fast," she admitted. "Had I not stopped we might have had a tie!" Then she turned to her father. "Father," she announced, "let us set the date for our wedding."

(9) So Atalanta happily wed Hippomenes, and from then on, they ran side by side.

4. Which is a metaphor?
   a. as fast as lightning
   b. she ran down a mountain path
   c. there lived in Greece
   d. she was the wind

5. Which is NOT a simile?
   a. as mad as a wet hen
   b. about as welcome as a skunk at an outdoor party
   c. use them wisely
   d. cunning as a fox

6. The author uses the metaphor *you are the sun in my sky* to show that
   a. the king loves his daughter.
   b. the castle has a skylight.
   c. Atalanta wants to marry a scientist.
   d. the king doesn't care about Atalanta.

7. Which includes a simile?
   a. threw it so far off the path
   b. he crossed the finish line
   c. he took one look
   d. he took off like a rocket

8. What does the simile *cold as ice* mean?
   a. friendly and polite
   b. not very polite or friendly
   c. requires refrigeration
   d. can be easily melted

PRACTICE 3: SIBLING SUPPORT

Read the selection, and then answer the questions that follow.

(1)   Mom says I'm old enough to help take care of my little brother, Andy. I'm
       down with that. He's an all right kid. Oh, sometimes he drools all over my
       homework or gets his sticky fingerprints all over my science project or tries
       to chew my MP3 player, but that's okay. . . . He's just a baby. Andy's a
       sponge, soaking up all the information he can about the world around him.

(2) Yesterday, while Mom is feeding Andy, the phone rings. "Honey, can you get that, please?" Mom yells. "I'm in the middle of feeding the baby."

(3) "Sure, Mom," I say, and I run to pick up the phone. It's my aunt, calling from California. Now I'm in the middle. You know, Aunt Mara tells me what to tell Mom and then Mom tells me what to say back. I feel like a tennis ball bouncing back and forth! Finally I yell, "Mom, please come talk to Aunt Mara and I'll feed Andy!"

(4) So, Mom takes the phone and hands me Andy's spoon and dish. "Thanks, Honey, you're such a big help," she says with a smile.

(5) In the kitchen, Andy's sitting in his highchair as quiet as a mouse, just waiting to be fed. I start to feed him like I've seen Mom do, saying, "Here comes the choo-choo!" while aiming a spoonful at his mouth. He opens his mouth, takes a spoonful of beets, then as explosive as an erupting volcano, he shoots it back at me! Now I have beets running down my cheeks like raindrops! I put the spoon down and wipe my face. Andy picks up the spoon, digs into the dish of food, then PLOP! Beets shoot clear across the room into the sink. I'm thinking, *Wow, this kid is good! Maybe someday he'll be in the NBA!*

(6) Andy is a machine, throwing spoonful after spoonful. And before long, beets are everywhere. Sage, our cat, is a bolt of lightning ready to strike, leaping in to check out this unexpected food source in her territory. One sniff convinces her that what's on the floor, which is now as slippery as an eel, isn't the good stuff!

(7) Now, Mom walks back into the room and slips on a pile of beets! She looks up at me, also as red as a beet. We both look at Andy, looking as cute as a button and saying as clear as a bell, "Beets!" Mom and I laugh, happy to know that Andy's learned a new word. Then, of course, we have to clean up the room . . . and ourselves. Andy? He just gurgles and drools some more, then curls up in his crib for a nap, snug as a bug in a rug!

9. The author uses the metaphor *Andy is a sponge* to explain that
   a. he drools a lot.
   b. he throws his food.
   c. he takes in, or learns, new things.
   d. he has learned to feed himself.

10. Which simile explains how the author felt, caught in the middle of a conversation?

    a. as snug as a bug in a rug

    b. as clear as a bell

    c. as happy as a clam

    d. like a tennis ball

11. The author used the metaphor *a bolt of lightning, ready to strike* to describe

    a. the mother.

    b. Sage.

    c. the author.

    d. Andy.

12. Which is a simile?

    a. quiet as a mouse

    b. as explosive as an erupting volcano

    c. beets running down my cheeks like raindrops

    d. all of the above

13. Which is NOT a metaphor *or* simile?

    a. Andy is a machine.

    b. red as a beet

    c. slips on a pile of beets

    d. as slippery as an eel

ANSWERS

1. b
2. c
3. b
4. d
5. c
6. a
7. d
8. b
9. c
10. d
11. b
12. d
13. c

P O S T T E S T

NOW THAT YOU have completed the 30 lessons, it's time to find out how much you've improved! The posttest that follows has 30 multiple-choice questions about the topics covered in the 30 lessons. Circle the answers to each question if this book belongs to you. If it doesn't, write the numbers 1–30 on a paper and record your answers there.

When you finish the test, check the answers on page 279. If you still had trouble with some questions, check out the lesson(s) listed with it. Reread the materials and try the posttest again!

"THE VILLAGE BLACKSMITH"

Excerpted from the poem by Henry Wadsworth Longfellow

Read the selection, and then answer the questions that follow.

> Under a spreading chestnut-tree
> The village smithy stands;
> The smith, a mighty man is he,
> With large and sinewy hands;
> And the muscles of his brawny arms
> Are strong as iron bands.
>
> His hair is crisp, and black, and long,
> His face is like the tan;
> His brow is wet with honest sweat,
> He earns whate'er he can,
> And looks the whole world in the face,
> For he owes not any man.
>
> Week in, week out, from morn till night,
> You can hear his bellows blow;
> You can hear him swing his heavy sledge,
> With measured beat and slow,
> Like a sexton ringing the village bell,
> When the evening sun is low.
>
> And children coming home from school
> Look in at the open door;
> They love to see the flaming forge,
> And hear the bellows roar,
> And catch the burning sparks that fly
> Like chaff from a threshing-floor.
>
> Toiling,—rejoicing,—sorrowing,
> Onward through life he goes;
> Each morning sees some task begin,
> Each evening sees it close;
> Something attempted, something done,
> Has earned a night's repose.

1. You can tell this is a poem because it
   a. tries to persuade readers to become blacksmiths.
   b. tells about a time in U.S. history.
   c. explains how to shoe a horse.
   d. has definite rhythm and a rhyme scheme.

2. The phrase *strong as iron bands* is an example of
   a. personification.
   b. hyperbole.
   c. simile.
   d. inference.

3. Which helps you know the poem is told from a third-person point of view?
   a. the pronouns *he* and *his*
   b. the verb *love*
   c. the pronouns *I* and *me*
   d. the noun *forge*

4. Context clues help you know that the word *repose* means
   a. swing.
   b. toil.
   c. sleep.
   d. rejoice.

5. Which line from the poem is the best example of imagery?
   a. He earns whate'er he can.
   b. Like chaff from a threshing-floor.
   c. For he owes not any man.
   d. His hair is crisp, and black, and long.

THE LIFELESS LAKES

Read the article, and then answer the questions that follow.

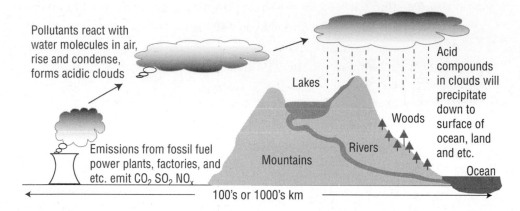

Pollutants react with water molecules in air, rise and condense, forms acidic clouds

Lakes

Acid compounds in clouds will precipitate down to surface of ocean, land and etc.

Woods

Rivers

Emissions from fossil fuel power plants, factories, and etc. emit CO_2 SO_2 NO_x

Mountains

Ocean

100's or 1000's km

(1)   In the early 1960s, people in Sweden noticed that something was terribly wrong. There were no more fish in some lakes where fish had always been abundant. In fact, there were no living organisms in the water at all! Scientists called the lakes "dead." By the 1970s, the problem had spread to some lakes in the northeastern United States.

Searching for Answers

(2)   Scientists tested the lake water and found it very acid . . . sometimes as acid as vinegar! No water animals or plants could survive in it. Scientists wondered if acid could possibly have dropped from the sky. They tested rainwater and other forms of precipitation. Each had a high level of acid.

(3)   Further study proved that "acid rain" was first discovered in the 1870s. A scientist in Scotland had found that coal smoke in the region made lake water acidic. Gases emitted by the burning coal had mixed with moisture in the air, then dropped to Earth in rain. Over the years, more coal-burning factories were built and more acid rain produced. But not all was caused by burning coal. Exhaust from modern vehicles also spewed acid into the air.

What Could Be Done?

(4)   In the United States, Congress passed Clean Air laws to reduce acid rain. Factories were to install "scrubbers" in smokestacks to remove acid particles before they got into the air. And vehicles had to pass yearly emissions tests. But some air pollution wasn't created here; it floated our way.

(5)   In recent years, China has built many coal-burning plants as it expands
      trade with other nations. The smoke drifts over China, then wind sweeps
      it across the ocean to other places, like the U.S. west coast. Many people are
      working to find ways to cut down on polluting gases in the air. I hope they
      succeed before we "kill" more lakes or streams!

6. The author probably wrote this article to
   a. teach readers how to test polluted water.
   b. explain to readers what acid rain is.
   c. entertain readers with a humorous tale.
   d. persuade readers to study science.

7. Which text feature does the author use to divide the article into sections?
   a. contents
   b. glossary
   c. index
   d. subheads

8. The author organizes the ideas in this article by
   a. telling a problem, then explaining some solutions.
   b. ranking ideas in the order of their importance.
   c. asking questions, then answering those questions.
   d. comparing and contrasting ideas.

9. From information in the article, you might conclude that
   a. the problem is now under control.
   b. most acid rain is caused by human activity.
   c. scientists don't know how the acid gets into the air.
   d. forest fires are caused by acid rain.

10. With which topic would you most likely use the term *precipitation*?
   a. computer animation
   b. ballroom dancing
   c. weather forecasting
   d. fashion design

11. The last sentence is an opinion, not a fact, because
   a. it talks about imaginary places.
   b. it's short.
   c. it can be proved true in an encyclopedia.
   d. it's what the author thinks.

12. How does the graphic help readers better understand the text?

    a. It's a map that shows where the dead lakes are located in Sweden.

    b. It's a diagram that explains how acid rain forms.

    c. It's a chart that lists the gases in acid rain.

    d. It's a photograph that shows automobile exhaust in the air.

PYGMALION

Excerpted and adapted from the play by George Bernard Shaw

Read the selection, and then answer the questions that follow.

    Act V: The parlor of Mrs. Higgins' home

MRS. HIGGINS: Now, Henry: be good.

HIGGINS: I am behaving myself perfectly. [*A pause. Higgins throws back his head; stretches out his legs; and begins to whistle.*]

MRS. HIGGINS: Henry, dearest, you don't look at all nice in that attitude.

HIGGINS [*pulling himself together*]: I was not trying to look nice, Mother. Where is that girl? Are we to wait here all day?

[*Eliza enters, carrying a little work-basket, and is very much at home.*]

ELIZA: How do you do, Professor Higgins? Are you quite well?

HIGGINS: [*choking*] Am I . . . [*He can say no more.*]

ELIZA: But of course you are: You are never ill. Quite chilly this morning, isn't it? [*She sits and begins to do needlework from her basket.*]

MRS. HIGGINS: Very nicely put, indeed, Henry.

HIGGINS: She has no idea I didn't put into her head or word I didn't put into her mouth! And now she pretends to play the fine lady with me?

MRS. HIGGINS [*kindly*]: Yes, dear; but you'll sit down, won't you?

[*Higgins sits down again, savagely.*]

ELIZA: You see, Mrs. Higgins, it was very difficult for me to learn, with the example of Professor Higgins, unable to control myself, and using bad language at the drop of a hat. I'd never have known how ladies and gentlemen behave if Colonel Pickering hadn't been there.

HIGGINS: Well!!

ELIZA: Do you know what began my real education? It was when Colonel Pickering calling me Miss Doolittle the first day I was at Wimpole Street. That was the beginning of self-respect for me. And little things that came naturally to him, like standing when I entered a room, showed me that he thought of me as something better than a flower girl. Professor Higgins never saw that the difference between a lady and a flower girl is not *how* she behaves, but how she's *treated*.

HIGGINS [*angrily*]: My manners are exactly the same as Colonel Pickering's!

ELIZA: That's not true. He treats a flower girl as if she was a duchess.

HIGGINS: And I treat a duchess as if she was a flower girl! [*Seriously*] The great secret, Eliza, is not in having bad manners or good manners, but having the same manner for all humans. I know sometimes I may seem to be an old bear, but the question is not whether I treat you rudely, but whether you've ever heard me treat anyone else better.

ELIZA [*with sudden sincerity*]: I don't care how you treat me. I don't mind your bad temper. But [*standing up and facing him*] I won't be passed over!

HIGGINS: Then get out of my way; for I won't stop for you. You talk about me as if I were a motor bus!

ELIZA: So you are a motor bus: all bounce and go, and no consideration for anyone! But I can do without you. . . . Don't think I can't!

HIGGINS: I know you can . . . but can I do without YOU?

ELIZA: You will have to. I will become a teacher. I'll put an ad in the paper that the girl everyone thinks is a duchess is only a flower girl that you taught, and she can teach anyone to be a duchess, too, in just six months!

HIGGINS [*smiling*]: By George, Eliza, I like you like this!

13. What is the tone of the selection?
   a. funny
   b. serious
   c. whimsical
   d. scientific

14. The denotation of *bear* is "a large mammal with long, shaggy hair." The connotation in this selection is
   a. "able to carry weight."
   b. "musical ability."
   c. "a kind of language."
   d. "a gruff, bad-mannered person."

15. As used in the selection, the meaning of the word *well* is
   a. "fountain of water."
   b. "in good health."
   c. "clearly."
   d. "fill up."

16. Which is an idiom?
    a. "treat a duchess"
    b. "very nicely put"
    c. "at the drop of a hat"
    d. "I can be a lady"

17. The theme of this play is
    a. "You should treat all people the same."
    b. "Beauty is only skin deep."
    c. "It's important to have a hobby, like needlepoint."
    d. "Save a penny for a rainy day."

18. The prefix *un-* in *unable* changes the base word to mean
    a. able to do again.
    b. full of ability.
    c. not capable of.
    d. before moving.

19. From what you read in this script, you can infer that
    a. Professor Higgins taught his mother how to act like a duchess.
    b. Professor Higgins taught Pickering how to act like a colonel.
    c. Professor Higgins taught Eliza how to do needlepoint.
    d. Professor Higgins taught Eliza how to speak and act like a duchess.

THE NOSE KNOWS!

Read the article, and then answer the questions that follow.

(1)   The giant anteater lives in forests and on the prairies of tropical South America. The hairy mammal feeds primarily on termites and other ants. The anteater's coat blends with the brownish grasses in which termites build nests. Just one anteater can devour 30,000 termites a day! The long-snouted predator has no teeth, but the way it eats, it doesn't need them!

(2)   When an anteater's hungry, it uses its long hooked claws to slash an opening in the nearest termite nest. Next, the anteater slides its long nose into the opening and sticks out its tongue, which is two feet (60 cm) long and coated with gooey saliva. Then, the predator takes a deep breath. As if

pulled by a vacuum cleaner, termites are sucked onto that dangerously gluey tongue. Finally, the anteater pulls its termite-covered tongue back into its mouth and eats the tasty insects. In just one minute, an anteater's tongue can enter and exit a termite nest more than 100 times!

20. Which best describes how the author organizes the information?
    a. by explaining a problem and suggesting solutions
    b. by comparing and contrasting objects
    c. by telling the events in sequence, or time order
    d. by giving facts and opinions

21. The words *Nose* and *Knows* in the title are
    a. synonyms.
    b. antonyms.
    c. homographs.
    d. homophones.

22. What is the main idea of this selection?
    a. Vacuum cleaners use suction to suck up materials.
    b. An anteater uses its nose and tongue to capture prey.
    c. Some anteaters are the size of a squirrel; giant anteaters may measure seven feet (2.1 m).
    d. Scientists know very little about anteaters.

SIBLING RIVALRY

Read the selection, and then answer the questions that follow.

(1) "There's going to be a kite-flying contest!" my little sister Allie yelled as she ran into the house. "I saw the sign in the drug store window!"

(2) "Great, another contest I can win!" I replied, not too humbly.

(3) "If we make a kite together, we both can win!" she said with a smile.

(4) "No, thanks," I snickered. "I'll make my own. I make a pretty mean box kite!"

(5) Allie's small face clouded with a look of disappointment. "Okay, I'll build my own kite," she mumbled. "Maybe I'll even win a prize!"

(6) The next afternoon, I saw Allie reading a library book. Around her on the floor were sticks, paper, glue, and string. *Oh, no!* I thought. *She's making an old-fashioned, two-stick paper kite!* I laughed as I went to work on my box kite.

(7) Right before the contest, I took my kite for a test run, and after a few seconds, it caught the wind and soared higher and higher. "Perfect! Behold the winner!" I said to my friend, Kyle.

(8) "Aren't you afraid of Allie?" laughed Kyle. "She always plays to win!"

(9) "Oh, yeah, I'm shaking in my boots!" I said as I reeled in my kite. Then a sudden gust of wind grabbed it and sent it spinning toward the ground. The string caught on an old, rickety fence, and my kite fell to the ground just beyond. As I leaped over the fence, the wind unbalanced me. CRUNCH! My feet landed firmly on my kite and it cracked into a zillion pieces!

(10) "Oh, no!" Allie cried when she saw it. "The contest's about to start! I know it's important to you, so if you want to . . . you can use my kite!"

(11) For a minute, believe me, I was tempted. Then I remembered how hard she'd worked to make her kite because I wouldn't help her. "Thanks, Allie," I said, "but you deserve the chance to compete."

(12) The contest began. One by one, kites caught the wind and climbed. The wind grew stronger. Box kites swerved crazily and fell to the ground. Even flat, plastic kites fell. Soon just one kite remained . . . Allie's. She'd won!

(13) I cheered along with the crowd. I really felt proud of Allie. "That's my little sister," I told people standing near me. "She made that kite all by herself!"

23. Which word is a synonym for *snickered*?
   a. sobbed
   b. laughed
   c. whimpered
   d. wrote

24. Which describes one of Allie's character traits?
   a. She likes to eat hot dogs.
   b. She has lived in the same house all her life.
   c. She really cares about her big brother.
   d. She doesn't like being around other people.

25. The narrator's kite was ruined because
   a. it fell into the lake.
   b. the wind blew it high up into a tree.
   c. Allie forgot to reel it in.
   d. the narrator accidentally jumped on it.

26. The line, *"Behold the winner," I said to my friend, Kyle,* foreshadowed that
   a. Kyle would win the contest.
   b. the narrator probably wasn't going to win.
   c. Allie had gone missing.
   d. the contest would be cancelled.

27. What is the main conflict in the story?
   a. Allie needs to go to the drug store to buy glue.
   b. Allie and the narrator need to earn money for kite supplies.
   c. Allie and the narrator both want to win the contest.
   d. Allie and Kyle both want the last sandwich.

HAVE YOUR SAY

Read the selection, and then answer the questions that follow.

(1) It's September. It's great to see our friends again, but wasn't it nice to have the summer off? Well, some folks think our school should be open all year. Wait! You wouldn't actually go to school every day, but your life might be pretty different!

(2) Not everyone agrees that an all-year school is a good idea. Those who do agree say kids forget a lot of what they learned over the long vacation, and it would be better to have more, shorter vacations. For example, we would have eight-week grading periods, followed by a week off. People who don't like the idea say the way we've been doing things for years is just fine, thank you very much. No need to change now! Besides, the longer summer vacation lets kids spend time with families and friends and get out into the fresh air! Also, they say, most parents have their vacations in summer, so a change in the school year would upset family plans.

(3) What's your take on the idea? For it? Against it? Let your opinion be heard. Send an e-mail to the school paper . . . today!

28. The author probably wrote this article to
    a. inform readers about a trip taken during summer vacation.
    b. teach readers how to plan a vacation.
    c. entertain readers with mystery.
    d. persuade readers to write e-mails to voice their opinions.

29. Which antonym pair was used in the selection?
    a. *summer* and *winter*
    b. *longest* and *shortest*
    c. *oldest* and *newest*
    d. *open* and *closed*

30. Which is the best one-sentence summary for this selection?
    a. All the parents want to have an all-year school.
    b. None of the parents wants to have an all-year school.
    c. People are discussing the possibility of having an all-year school.
    d. Students are not allowed to voice their opinions in school.

ANSWERS

If you miss a question, look for help with that topic in the lesson(s) listed.

1. d (Lesson 8)
2. c (Lesson 30)
3. a (Lesson 25)
4. c (Lesson 6)
5. d (Lesson 27)
6. b (Lesson 9)
7. d (Lesson 11)
8. a (Lessons 16, 18, 19)
9. b (Lesson 21)
10. c (Lesson 5)
11. d (Lesson 17)
12. b (Lesson 12)
13. b (Lesson 10)
14. d (Lesson 7)
15. b (Lesson 1)
16. c (Lesson 29)
17. a (Lesson 26)
18. c (Lesson 4)
19. d (Lesson 20)
20. c (Lessons 14, 16, 17, 19)
21. d (Lesson 2)
22. b (Lesson 13)
23. b (Lesson 3)
24. c (Lesson 23)
25. d (Lesson 15)
26. b (Lesson 28)
27. c (Lesson 24)
28. d (Lesson 9)
29. b (Lesson 3)
30. c (Lesson 22)

antonym   a word that means the opposite of another word

author's purpose   an author's reason for writing a selection: to explain, teach, entertain, or persuade

base word   a word that can stand alone to which a prefix or suffix is added

cause and effect   what makes something happen and what does happen

character   a person, an animal, or an object in a story

chronological order text structure   organizes ideas in time order, or sequence

compare-and-contrast text structure   organizes ideas by telling how things are alike or different

conclusion   a decision based on given facts

conflict and resolution   a character's problem and how it is solved

connotation   a feeling or image a word brings to mind

context clues   other words in the text that help readers figure out unknown words

denotation   the dictionary definition of a word

fact-and-opinion text structure   organizes ideas by giving facts, details that can be proven true, and opinions or what someone thinks

fiction   a story made up by the author

figurative language   words that do not always mean exactly what they say

first-person point of view   story told by one of the characters

flashback   an interruption in a story to explain what had happened in the past

foreshadowing   clues about what might happen later in a story

genre   a kind of fiction or nonfiction

graphics   features that give information visually

heading   the name of a chapter or section

homograph   two words spelled the same but pronounced differently and with different meanings

homophone   two words that sound alike but are spelled differently and have different meanings

hyperbole   exaggeration to make a point

idiom   a word or group of words that doesn't mean exactly what it says

imagery   words that help readers create pictures in their minds

inference   a logical guess based on facts and personal experiences

jargon   special language used by people who work together or do things as a group

main idea   what a selection is mostly about

metaphor   a figure of speech that compares two things by stating that one thing is, or has the characteristics of, another

multiple-meaning word   a word that means more than one thing

narrator   the person telling a story

nonfiction   information about the real world

novel   a book of fiction divided into chapters

personification   language that gives human qualities to animals or objects

plot   what happens in a story

poetry fiction with rhythm and often a rhyme scheme

prefix letters added to the beginning of a word to change its meaning

problem-and-solution text structure organizes ideas by telling about a problem and suggesting solutions

question-and-answer text structure organizes ideas by asking a question and providing the answer either right there in the text of through a series of details

root a Latin or Greek word part that can't stand alone

setting where and when a story takes place

simile compares two things, using the word *like* or *as*

style an author's distinctive way of connecting ideas

subhead names a smaller part within a chapter or section

suffix letters added to the end of a word to change its meaning

summary a short retelling of a story or event

supporting detail tells more about the main idea

synonym a word that has the same meaning as another word

text features headings, subheads, and special text that help readers find information in a selection

theme the most important idea or message

third-person point of view story told by a noncharacter

tone conveys a feeling, like suspense, excitement, happiness, sadness, anger, mystery, humor, or annoyance